# THE FATE OF MAN

# H. G. WELLS

# THE FATE OF MAN

*An unemotional Statement of the Things that are happening to him now, and of the immediate Possibilities confronting him*

*Essay Index Reprint Series*

 **BOOKS FOR LIBRARIES PRESS**
FREEPORT, NEW YORK

College Library, Wayne, Nebr.

First Published 1939
Reprinted 1970

STANDARD BOOK NUMBER:
8369-1487-2

LIBRARY OF CONGRESS CATALOG CARD NUMBER:
70-105049

PRINTED IN THE UNITED STATES OF AMERICA

## CONTENTS

| | PAGE |
|---|---|
| INTRODUCTION | 1 |

CHAPTER
1. PRELIMINARY STATEMENT . . . . . . . . . 15
2. BIOLOGY INVADES HISTORY . . . . . . . . 18
3. HOW SPECIES SURVIVE . . . . . . . . . . 21
4. HISTORY BECOMES ECOLOGY . . . . . . . 27
5. UNION NOW? . . . . . . . . . . . . . . 39
6. WHAT IS DEMOCRACY? . . . . . . . . . . 44
7. WHERE IS DEMOCRACY? . . . . . . . . . 58
8. WHAT MAN HAS TO LEARN . . . . . . . . 64
9. SAMPLE OF A GENERATION . . . . . . . . 65
10. ESTIMATING HOPE . . . . . . . . . . . . 85
11. SURVEY OF EXISTING FORCES . . . . . . . 93
12. THE JEWISH INFLUENCE . . . . . . . . . 102
13. CHRISTENDOM . . . . . . . . . . . . . 118
14. WHAT IS PROTESTANTISM? . . . . . . . . 134

## CONTENTS

| CHAPTER | | PAGE |
|---|---|---|
| 15. | THE NAZI RELIGION | 142 |
| 16. | TOTALITARIANISM | 151 |
| 17. | THE BRITISH OLIGARCHY | 155 |
| 18. | SHINTOISM | 167 |
| 19. | THE CHINESE OUTLOOK | 175 |
| 20. | SUBJECT PEOPLES | 189 |
| 21. | COMMUNISM AND RUSSIA | 197 |
| 22. | AMERICAN MENTALITY | 210 |
| 23. | THREE FACTORS IN EVERYONE | 226 |
| 24. | SUMMARY | 230 |
| 25. | IMPOSSIBILITY OF UTOPIANISM | 232 |
| 26. | DECADENT WORLD | 235 |
|  | NOTES | 249 |

# THE FATE OF MAN

## INTRODUCTION

I HAVE BEEN ASKED to set down as simply and clearly as I can, in one compact book, the reality of the human situation; that is to say I have been asked to state the world as I see it and what is happening to it. This is the result.

A very large part of my conscious life has been a struggle for effective knowledge. I have attempted to collect and summarize existing knowledge so that it could be made available in human living, and to induce other and abler people to take up the same work. I have worked also to bring together incompatible systems of thinking about reality, systems which ignore each other stupidly and wastefully, and are manifestly answerable for much fundamental confusion in human thought. These unresolved, contradictory philosophies and theologies encumber the human mind, and their irresolution is largely due to an elaborate mutual disregard. I am exceptionally intolerant of such inconsistencies, because if I attempt to deal with them they worry and entangle me. I cannot make the necessary reservations and adjustments.

The peculiar strength and the peculiar weakness of my mind are one and the same quality. Put favorably, mine is a very direct mind; put unfavorably, it is unsubtle. I am impatient of complicating details and conventional misstatements because I am afraid of them. The reader will find this book ego-centered, for so we all began, and also insistent. I *hammer* at my main ideas, and this is an offense to delicate-minded people. If a door is not open I say it is shut, and I am impatient with the suggestion of worldly wisdom that it may be possible to wangle a way round. Yet there may be a way round if you do not lose yourself getting there. You have been warned that I shall not be with you in any such uncertain enterprise. I work not simply for knowledge but for a stark clarity of thought about it. It seems to me a fair challenge to demand a lucid statement of the vision of the universe to which this directness of inquiry and assemblage have brought me.

That vision may affect many readers as unflattering to human self-esteem. I cannot help that; it is the way in which reality has unfolded itself before me.

By way of Introduction I will tell how I came to see the world as I do. Then in the subsequent sections I will give the conclusions at which I have arrived today. I will tell what I first saw of life. How I saw it. How I was allowed to see it. How my range of vision extended. How knowledge, experience and imagination accumulated and horizon opened beyond horizon.

I was born in a rather unprosperous home; there was no nursery and most of my waking day was spent in an underground kitchen. Very little remains in my memory now of that first world, my infantile world. As I saw it then, it seemed to be the only world. When I put together the notes for this Introduction, I sat for a time, doing my utmost to recall what picture of the world I had in early childhood. I get scarcely anything at all.

It must have been a very limited picture. I had few general ideas. Or none. For instance, my mind was not living in a flat world or a round world or anything of that sort. I was not bothering about any shape or size of the world. I was entirely incurious about all that. I was just living in *"the* world." I was informed that there was a home for little children above the bright blue sky, but I do not remember that that interested me in the slightest degree. I was rather more concerned about Old Bogey who would come and fetch me if I told fibs and so on, and I rather disliked (but I did not think very much about) a certain divine eye that was always watching me—generally with disapproval. But as far as my recollections go, I was much more afraid of bears, tigers, black men, red Indians and other dangers, lurking in the shadows upstairs and round the corner. That infantile world was a world of vivid, immediate, inconsecutive realities against a background of nothingness that evoked no curiosity. There was the house next door, there was the moon, there was night, there was day and so forth. Why not? With the utmost effort, that is all I can reconstruct of the world I saw before I began to read books and see pictures, go for walks, go to school, and inspect and inquire with the freedom of seven or eight years old.

I have a fuller conception of what I was seeing after that stage. My imagination was being used to amplify and extend what I saw and heard and felt directly. A rather foggy time-background was taking shape. I heard about "Once upon a time," before I existed. I had a jumbled idea of old England, mostly forests with turrets peeping out of them, old Paris, Rome, where it was always Nero and Christians fighting beasts in the Coliseum. My historical ideas centered upon Windsor Castle. I had seen Windsor Castle, and I firmly believed that that grandiose round tower, which George the Fourth clapped upon it, was built by William the Conqueror. Rome, Greece, Babylon, Jerusalem and Egypt, arranged anyhow, crowded the background, and the Creation, seen across the shining waters of the Flood and a curious procession of very, very, very old gentlemen—Methuselah beat the record—sealed up the vista of the past.

I was interested in geography chiefly because it provided varied scenery for imaginary adventures. I thought China and Japan were made to be laughed at, though their porcelain and silks and fans were clever. I knew that there were also savages for whom Britain provided missionaries and machine-guns. Savages were generally cannibals and wore few or no garments, which seemed to me very rude of them indeed. I knew the world was round because everybody told me so. If they had told me the world was cone-shaped or flat, I should have known that with equal conviction—and it was only years afterwards that I realized how difficult it is to prove that the world is a globe. There were upper classes one respected and lower classes that one didn't, and poor people had to work, and that was how things were. The nearer I could edge up to the upper classes the better it would be for me.

So I saw the world about the year 1880, when I was rising fourteen years old, and I think most of my readers will agree with me that I was seeing the world then in a very distorted and foggy fashion. And yet—I was seeing it as most people in Great Britain were seeing it at that time. I was seeing it as vast multitudes of people are seeing it today. I was seeing it as it was shown to me. For a score of years before that time tremendous discoveries had been made about the past of the earth and about the origins of man. They were immensely important discoveries, they were a challenge to every idea about life commonly accepted at that time. Yet these fundamental discoveries had not been imparted to my parents, who were both intelligent, book-reading persons. My lay and religious teachers, poor men, bound in honor, you would have thought, to teach me the truth, the whole truth and nothing but the truth, gave me their stale old histories without a hint of the broadening knowledge of the time. I still wonder why they deceived me so. Mainly I think because they were too overworked and underpaid to keep up with the times. They couldn't tell me because they themselves had not been told about these revelations. They were the ignorant, self-satisfied transmitters of a dead tradition.

Most of the books that came into my hands were books ten or twenty years old, for in those days, just as now, no one, no education minister for example, was pretending to dream of giving people contemporary knowledge. Even today, except for a few rare adventurous publishers, nobody in any country in the world is really bothering to secure mankind abundant, cheap, new books. Cheap new books happen or don't happen according to the state of the market. Knowledge oozes about with cheap printing and paper, and dries up when they dry up. Our English-speaking democracies, about which we boast so inordinately, are still grossly ignorant and misinformed. But I think the books we got in 1880 were more second-hand and out-of-date and shabbier than the stuff people get today. So by 1880 I saw my world pretty wrong—by the higher standards of that time.

I forget when it was I began to realize that the world as it had been presented to me was not a trustworthy picture of reality, that in effect I was being lied to about life. I began doubting quite early in life. The religion they put before me was queer, muddled stuff, metaphors about unfatherly fathers and sacrificial sons, blood offerings and blood-dripping sacrificial lambs (in suburban London!), an irrational fall and a vindictive judgment, stuff that took refuge from any intelligent questions behind a screen of awe, mystery and menace, so that my reason did not so much reject it as fail altogether to accept it. What they called morality seemed planned to thrust me into some nasty secret corners and leave me there. I had some bad times, fearing a God whom I felt but did not dare to think a spy, a bully, a tyrant and fundamentally insane, and it was only after terrific distresses and terrors that I achieved disbelief. Fear lingered in my mind long after definite faith had dissolved.

The sublunary world they imposed upon me was equally difficult to accept. The history they taught me wound up at 1700, which was queer when one came to think about it. But even then I must have read books about the French Revolution and George Washington and the Roman Republic, and they had upset my simple faith in the inevitability of our political order, the dear Queen and all the rest of it. A sixpenny book by the late Henry George came into my hands and set me thinking crudely, destructively, but profitably about rent, wages and suchlike matters. Some rumors about a science called geology reached me. I had already observed for myself in the pictures in Wood's *Natural History* that different species of animals had quite needless resemblances to one another, if it was indeed true that they had all been made separately. Then about that time my schoolmaster set me reading science textbooks to earn Education Department grants for him, and suddenly I woke up to the existence of a vast and growing world of thought and knowledge outside my ordinary circle of ideas altogether. My heavens opened, and the world as I had seen it hitherto became a flimsy veil upon the face of reality.

I have heard other people who have had similar experiences to mine tell of the *thirst for knowledge* they experienced. I suppose I had that thirst in good measure, but far stronger was my anger at the paltry sham of an education that had been fobbed off upon me; angry resentment also at the dismal negligence of the social and religious organizations responsible for me, that had allowed me to be thrust into the hopeless drudgery of a shop, ignorant, misinformed, undernourished and physically under-developed, without warning and without guidance, at the age of thirteen. To sink or swim. I was too young to make allowances for the people who were exploiting and stifling me. I did not realize that they were quite charming people really, if a little too self-satisfied and indolent. I thought they had conspired to keep me down. It wasn't true that they had conspired to keep me down. But I was down and they didn't bother. They took my inferiority as part of the accepted order. They just trod on me. But I did not discriminate about their responsibility. I *hated* them as only the young can hate, and it gave me the energy to struggle, and I set about struggling, for knowledge. I was bitterly determined to see my world clearer and truer, before it was too late.

To this day I will confess I dislike the restriction and distortion of knowledge as I dislike nothing else on earth. In this modern world it is, I hold, second only to murder to starve and cripple the mind of a child. Emasculation of the mind is surely more horrible than any degrading bodily mutilation. In our modern world we recoil from the deliberate manufacture of human dwarfs, harem attendants and choristers, but the world still swarms with mental cripples, who follow the laws of their own distortion and scarcely suspect they are distorted.

I have indicated the limits of my world outlook in 1880. By extraordinary good luck I caught up to something like contemporary knowledge in the course of a few years. In seven years, before I was twenty-one, I contrived—never mind how—to secure four years of almost continuous study, and three of these were at the Royal College of Science, and one under the professorship of the great Huxley, Darwin's friend; and by 1887 the world as I saw it had become something altogether greater, deeper and finer than the confused picture I had of it in 1880. Mentally, we all travel at our fastest, I suppose, between fourteen and twenty-one. Many of my readers will know from their own experience what I mean when I say that for me these years remain in my memory as if all the time I was putting together an immense jig-saw puzzle in a mood of inspiration. These were the most exciting years in my life. I had been blind and I was learning to see. The world opened out before me. By '88 I saw the world, not precisely as I see it today, but much more as I see it today than as I saw it in 1880. There has been a lot of expansion and supplementing since, but nothing like a fundamental reconstruction.

Now how did we—because I was one of a generation of science students—how did we see the world in '88? Time

## INTRODUCTION

had opened out for us, and the Creation, the Fall of Man and the Flood, those simple fundamentals of the Judæo-Christian mythology, had vanished. Forever. Instead I saw a limitless universe throughout which the stars and nebulæ were scattering like dust, and I saw life ascending, as it seemed, from nothingness towards the stars.

In the eighties the prevailing ideas about space and time, matter and energy, were simpler than they are now. Space and time just went on forever, we thought. We students used to talk about the fourth and other dimensions, but when I wrote a story for the students' magazine and identified time with the fourth dimension, I thought I was being very original and paradoxical indeed. We also had very definitely limited ideas about the amount of energy latent in the universe, and it seemed to us that our world would probably "freeze up" in a few million years. Still even that gave us a long time ahead, and we thought humanity might see and do tremendous things. We knew the broad outline of the history of life in time; we knew that our ancestors were apes, and it seemed possible that man would go on to a power and wisdom beyond all precedent.

But our ideas of that progress we anticipated were remarkably restricted. Our imaginations were relatively unstimulated. For example, our world, as we saw it then, knew nothing of radio—or to be exact it knew of radio transmission as a curious laboratory experiment, the Hertzian waves —and its ideas about atoms and the statement of physical processes, were naive in the extreme. We doubted if aviation was possible, we doubted if electric traction was possible, we associated submarines with the fantasies of Jules Verne, and we considered his *Around the World in Eighty*

*Days* an extravagant dream. Our interpretation of mental actions was trivial and shallow almost beyond comparison with what we have now.

As I compare the world as I see it now, with that world I contemplated fifty years ago, I realize how greatly the picture has unfolded and how much understanding has intensified. So far as its scale and texture go, so far as space and time, the atoms and the threads and substance of the picture go, the world as I see it today is altogether more marvelous, mysterious and profound.

It is not only that our analysis of the rhythms and interplay of the physical elements of the universe has been elaborated and rephrased in far more effective modes. In the foreground and middle distance also, concerning affairs upon this planet and the more obvious and immediate activities of life, our enlightenment has been immense. Thanks largely to Freud and his disciples and successors, there has been an immense advance in our self-knowledge. I would put Freud side by side with Darwin as a significant figure in human enlightenment. These two men are cardinal not so much on account of the actual elucidations they produced but because of the questions they asked and the method of their questioning. Our knowledge first of our own motives and impulses and then of mass-thought and mass-action, has become beyond comparison more lucid and practical, thanks primarily to the initiatives of Freud.

One immediate result of this rapid progressive enlargement and confirmation of our former outlook has been a tremendous wave of optimistic assurance in the minds of liberal-minded, freely thinking people. They have taken progress in discovery, in intelligent social organization, in the conquest of want, disease, ignorance, as something almost as inevitable as the precession of the Equinoxes. That progress has had the air of something quite independent of the daily lives and mass responses of everyday people. There was nothing anyone need do about it. It came; it unfolded; it increased. Progress! The men of science, the inventors, clever people somewhere were doing it all for us and all we had to do was to sit back and marvel and accept the cornucopia. There are the facts before us, the novelties, the triumphs, perpetually reinforced. In the world as I see it today, the powers and possibilities of human effort appear enormously greater than they did in 1888. And still they increase. Still the prospect and the promise expand.

The case for optimism about physical wants is stronger now than ever. So far as economic circumstances go, the world could be organized to provide every living soul upon it with abundant food, housing and leisure, and that without either direct compulsion to toil or any irksome monotony of employment. We have passed in a single lifetime from a general neediness to a practicable plenty for all. The story is too familiar to need exhaustive recapitulation here. Aviation and radio communication have abolished distance. In 1888 the unity of the world as one community was a remote aspiration; *now* it has become an imperative necessity. Fifty years ago none of us dreamt of the freedom and fullness of life that is now a plain possibility for everyone. To many hopeful people in the past few decades, an age of power, freedom and abundance has seemed close at hand. Eye has not seen nor ear heard, it is only now entering into the human imagination to conceive, the wonder of the years to come.

And now suddenly we are confronted by a series of distresses and disasters, of a nature to convince the most hopeful of us that all this happy assurance was premature. We anticipated too easily, too greedily and too uncritically. These new powers, inventions, contrivances and methods, are not the unqualified enrichment of normal life that we had expected. They are hurting, injuring and frustrating us increasingly. They are proving dangerous and devastating in our eager but unprepared hands. We are only beginning to realize that the cornucopia of innovation may perhaps prove far more dangerous than benevolent.

What we may call the scientific world has recognized this quite recently. There have been great stirrings of conscience in various scientific organizations upon the question of the misuse of science and invention, and how far the man of science may be held responsible for that misuse. The Associations for the Advancement of Science in Britain, America and Australia have been moving under the initiatives of such men as Sir Frederick Gowland Hopkins, Lord Rutherford and Sir Richard Gregory. The British Association has created a special Division, not merely a new section but a sort of collateral to itself, for the study of the social relations of science. The fate of this Division will be of considerable interest from our point of view. I have been privileged to attend some of its deliberations and two divergent lines of tendency have been very evident. One is plainly to organize and implement the common creative impulse in the scientific mind so as to make it a vital factor in public opinion; that was the original impulse which evoked the Division; the other is to restrain any such development of an authoritative and perhaps embarrassing criticism of the conduct of public affairs and to keep the man of science modestly to his present subordination.

It would carry us too far afield to discuss here how far the consciences of men of science may be able to get the upper hand of a trained and experienced governing class, so as to insist upon such collective ideals as they are able to formulate, and how far a trained and experienced governing class may maneuver this medley of distressed and protesting intelligences into the position of a roster of mere "experts" available if called upon by the authorities, and otherwise out of consideration.

It is conceivable that the scientific worker is even now walking into a net; that increasing areas of his inquiries and experiments are falling under the restrictions of "official secrets"; and that far beyond the more obvious realms of physics and chemistry, fields of investigation that have no direct bearing upon warfare are likely to come under control, as favoring subversive ideas undermining the military morale of the community. In Nazi Germany this has happened already to psychological science, to mathematical physics and ethnology—matters quite outside armament and strategy. An almost complete strangulation of the unhampered publication and exchanges of the free scientific period is visibly within the range of contemporary possibility, and the world of scientific workers, as we know them, even with that "Division" to rally them, appears a feeble folk to resist the influences making for that extinction.

No one has ever explored the bases of intellectual freedom in the modern community, and they may prove to be far more flimsy than the intellectual worker, flinging his mind about in the apparent security of his study, imagines.

It is not simply the forcible misuse of purely mechanical inventions that is producing such frightening retrogressions of those brave, free hopes that culminated in the later twenties. Every fresh development of radio, of the film and mass information generally, and all the new educational devices to which we had looked for the rapid spread of enlightenment and a common world understanding, are being subordinated more and more to government restriction and the service of propaganda. They were to have been the artillery of progress. They are rapidly being turned against our mental freedoms with increasing effectiveness.

Plainly, it is high time we looked more closely into the causes of these disconcerting frustrations of our recent large, bright anticipations of a world of plenty and expansion. What is the real position of *Homo sapiens* in relation to his environment? Has he the mastery we assumed he had, or did we make a profound miscalculation of his outlook? Have we been indulging in hopeful assumptions rather than facing the realities of his case? Upon that question the subsequent summary concentrates.

# 1

## PRELIMINARY STATEMENT

SINCE THE DAY WHEN Herbert Spencer launched the word "Sociology" upon the world, the study of the general question of *what is happening to mankind* has made great advances. Sociology—or, to give it a more recent and better name, human ecology—has become a real science, analyzing operating causes and forecasting events. Our awareness of our circumstances is altogether more lucid than the world outlook even of our fathers. We have, flowing into the problem of human society, a continually more acute analysis of its population movements, of its economic processes, of the relation of its activities to the actual resources available. We no longer talk with quite the same pompous ignorance as the history teachers of our youth, of the rise and decay of Empires and of the march of civilization from East to West—or from West to East, it is much the same—and suchlike plausible caricatures of the current of events. With the increase in our knowledge and understanding quite new conceptions of the prospects and problems of humanity unfold before us.

The infiltration of biological ideas into sociology and human history, it has to be recognized, is a process still only beginning. The enlightenment of the middle nineteenth century through the destructive analysis of the Creation myth, went on in the face of vast resistances, and not the least of these were in the schools. The new conceptions threatened the very bases of belief on which right conduct seemed to rest. Men shrank from following out the plain implications of the new discoveries. And so either they were denied, irrationally and frantically, or they were minimized, they were admitted, yes, but as obscure, remote matters, that had little or no significance in the "broader issues" of life. So that they could be taught in a sterilized form or ignored altogether. There was a period of controversy, very disastrous to the old dogmas, and then a phase of defensive silences. Open fighting was abandoned and the established beliefs dug themselves in.

It is still possible for bright youngsters at the universities to enter upon the "advanced" study of history, philosophy and economics, in the blackest ignorance of general biology. A majority of them remain in that ignorance, with a deepening scholastic hostility to this science, which sits like a neglected creditor at their doors. They have established a social prejudice against this dreaded line of thought and body of knowledge in which they have no share. They succeed in putting it upon the all too snobbish and sensitive young that somehow the biological reference is not quite the thing. It isn't *done*. It isn't to be thought about. There is an indecency in it. The young university philosopher, historian or economist is in many cases not so much biologically ignorant as biology-proofed.

It is because of such mental gaps and barriers that it is necessary to recapitulate here certain facts about life, which, although they are matters of general knowledge today be-

## PRELIMINARY STATEMENT

yond question and almost beyond cavil, might nevertheless, so far as any effective realization of their bearing upon our general social, political and religious behavior goes, be totally unknown. Yet they bear upon the problems of the present urgently. Contemporary political discussion remains indeed mere maundering empiricism, a tissue of guesses, ill-founded assertions and gossip, until they are brought into court.

This contrast of established knowledge and its effective application is a very remarkable one. Men can know a thing and yet know it quite ineffectively if it contradicts the general traditions and habits in which they live. It is well to understand that at this stage in our analysis, because it bears very directly upon the review of human possibilities to which this summary is directed.

2

## BIOLOGY INVADES HISTORY

ONE OF THE MOST striking differences between the outlook of our grandparents and that of a modern intelligence today is the modification of time values that has occurred.

By the measure of our knowledge their time-scale was extremely shallow. They had scarcely any historical perspective at all. They looked back to a past of a few thousand years and at the very *beginning* of time as they conceived it, they saw human life very much as it is now: it was a more or less balanced system of certain social types: rulers and ruled, hunter and cultivator, priest and soldier. This they regarded as the immemorial life of man. They saw the life of city and cultivated land, desert and sea, throughout all the interval, spreading perhaps, changing in a few particulars, enriched rather than altered by inventions and discoveries, but essentially the same. Their range of observation and comparison was too limited for them to realize that by clearing forests, overstocking grasslands, destroying soil, they were slowly impoverishing and devastating many of the regions into which they spread. They did not connect the rise and fall of empires with a factor of unforeseeing waste in that normal life of theirs. They ascribed such drifting of population and energy as they observed to other causes. These processes of primitive waste were too relatively slow to be perceptible from lifetime to lifetime. So these thinkers of yesterday talked of unchanging human nature. You cannot change human nature, they said. They relied upon the fabled promise of the rainbow, they had it straight from the Creator's mouth, that while the earth still remained, seedtime and harvest should endure.

The order of events seemed a sure, unfailing routine. And in much the same way, our ancestors, until a couple of dozen centuries ago, thought the world was flat. They thought the sea they sailed upon flat without qualification, and it required a considerable amount of mental exercise for them to realize that the apparent plane of the ocean surface was really curved and that the faster and farther they sailed the more effectively they would realize how the round earth was falling away from their first assumptions. All their old landmarks would then vanish one after another. Astounded navigators found unfamiliar constellations in the heavens. Within two dozen centuries man has been discovering that he lives not on a flat earth but upon a globe, and within the last ten, that he is not the center of the universe but a denizen of a very second-rate planet. He has had to readjust his general ideas about life to that, and to a certain extent he has adjusted them. To a certain extent only.

And similarly our historical imaginations, quite as much as our geographical imaginations, live today in a vastly enlarged system of perspectives. We know that the everlasting hills are not everlasting, that all our working conceptions of behavior and destiny are provisional and that human nature and everything about it is being carried along upon an irreversible process of change. Our historical ideas reach back now through vistas of millions of years, we see humanity emerging from sub-human conditions, from the life of relatively solitary apes, at distances in the nature of a quarter of a million years, we know with increasing precision of the onset of a social hunting life in those distant ages, we are able to trace the beginnings of agriculture in a period of two or three hundred centuries, and by the new scale, the development of cities, language, law, religious organization, and all the various adaptations of humanity to the new conditions of a regular food supply, all that social system which seemed as eternal as the heavens, appear now events of yesterday, devoid of any finality whatsoever. That fixity of the normal human life which our great-great-grandfathers assumed as a matter of plain common sense, we discover was a transient dream. As our perspectives open, it vanishes.

The rapid progress of social psychology, human ecology and all the ill-defined activities of human and general biology is opening our eyes, it is opening even the eyes of our trained historians and our social teachers, to the real nature of our everyday social life. It is brought home to us that the human species for the last twenty or twenty-five thousand years has been living in such a continuously accelerating process of change as no other animal species has ever been called upon to face. And it is also being forced upon our reluctant attention that the species *Homo sapiens* is no privileged exception to the general conditions that determine the destinies of other living species. It prospers or suffers under the same laws. These laws can be stated compactly, and there is nowadays very little dispute about them, even in matters of detail.

3

## HOW SPECIES SURVIVE

WHAT IN GENERAL TERMS are the relations of a species to the world about it?

A species may be living in practical harmony with its environment or it may be more or less out of balance with its surroundings.

In the former case it may continue recognizably the same species, living the same life, age after age. Any tendency to excessive numbers may be corrected by a correlated increase in the types that prey upon it, and there will be no definite biological encouragement for such variations and mutations as occur. Harmless mutations may indeed produce varieties and sub-species, and, as Henry Fairfield Osborn long ago pointed out, there may be purely mutational efflorescences; the correlation of a species to its environment is never hard and exact; but only a minority of mutations seem to be without some quality of advantage or disadvantage. Abnormal individuals in a species in practical equilibrium will generally be eliminated, and the species as a whole will pursue the even tenor of its way indefinitely.

There are species that have been under no necessity to adjust themselves to circumstances over vast periods of geological time. But they are exceptions to the general ecological spectacle of species balancing themselves in a changing world. Most existing species, when their affairs are scrutinized as a whole, are discovered to be in a state of imperfect adjustment to their circumstances, and to be either undergoing adaptation to meet new requirements or to be losing ground in the struggle—if one may call anything so essentially passive a struggle—to survive. Over a large part of the animal and vegetable kingdoms, adaptation, the working adjustment of the species under stress, is made, if it is made at all, by the selective frustration and killing off of less well-adjusted individuals. Variations and mutations—it is not necessary to enter here into the controversial question of their causes; suffice it that they occur—variations and mutations, indifferent, favorable and unfavorable, play a considerable part in this selective adjustment. The adjustment is either sufficient or insufficient. In the latter case, the species dwindles and disappears. In the former, the species undergoes modification; it survives, changed, as a new species or as several new species according to the imperatives of its altered conditions.

All this again is practically common knowledge today. Most educated people know about it even if they do not think very much about it, or link it up with other systems of ideas in their minds. It needs to be repeated plainly here in view of that possibility of disregard.

The general history of life in the past is, as everybody knows, one of failure and defeat rather than adaptation. Great groups of living things have arisen, had their heyday, and then passed altogether from the scene, giving place to more plastic and adaptable forms of life. Comparatively insignificant forms with novel accommodations arise to take their place.

When we contemplate that greater past that science has unfolded for us, we see great groups and orders of mighty creatures dominating the earth, enormous reptiles, huge mammals flourishing and then waning and passing away. They have not kept pace with change; their exuberance has been almost a defiance of change; and change has overcome and obliterated them. The geological record can be presented, certain assumptions being granted, as on the whole a great progression, but that does not alter the fact that it is also a history of the ruthless extinction of whole species, genera and orders of living things. There are tremendous massacres in the geological record.

One of the greatest of these occurred at the close of the Mesozoic period, when in the course of perhaps only a few hundred thousand years, a vast reptilian fauna, ichthyosaurus, plesiosaurus, tyrannosaurus and so forth, an equally wonderful flora, scores of genera of ammonites and so on and so forth, were thrust out of existence. We know little or nothing of the changes that made so many hitherto successful forms of life impossible. We know surely only that they occurred. A change from conditions of all-the-year-round equable temperature to wide seasonal alternations of heat and cold may have resulted from some planetary disturbance. More recently there have been parallel massacres of groups of the early mammals, and there can be no question that today we are, from the geological point of view, living in a phase of exceptional climatic instability, in a series of glacial and interglacial ages, and witnessing another destruction of animal and plant species on an almost unparalleled scale. The list of species extinguished in the past hundred years is a long one; the list of species threatened with extinction today is still longer. No new species arise to replace those exterminated. It is a swift, distressful impoverishment of life that is now going on. And this time the biologist notes a swifter and stranger agent of change than any phase of the fossil past can show—*man,* who will leave nothing undisturbed from the ocean bottom to the stratosphere, and who bids fair to extinguish himself in the process.

This species man is, as we all know, one of a great series of species which we can speak of roughly as cerebral animals. These are the mammals who have dominated the earth since the beginning of the Tertiary period and which display throughout a rapid development of the cerebral cortex. This cerebral cortex was a novelty in the history of life, and it brought with it a fresh, distinctive method of individual adaptation to special circumstances. It quickened the response of a species to changing conditions very greatly. Learning from experience appears indeed but very rudimentarily in cold-blooded vertebrata; it is only in the birds and mammals, and particularly in the latter, that it becomes of real importance in adaptation. Essentially the cerebrum is an organ for the storage and application of memories. It enables individuals to learn by experience. The history of the mammals in particular is a history of memory development. All through the Tertiary period, it is to be noted, brains in every group of mammals increase in relative size and complexity. With every increase, the power of learning from experience and of supplementing direct impulse by conditioned reflexes increases. A young fish or reptile comes into the world with a practically complete, almost unalterable set of instinctive responses. It survives or fails by its inherited outfit. Apparently it can learn to a certain extent, but it learns very little. A young mammal comes into life far less conclusively equipped, a *tabula rasa,* prepared to learn. It learns. And the ampler its cerebral equipment, the more it learns to take care of itself. To begin with, it is sillier and less certain than the cold-blooded type; it stands in need of protection; in the end it is far better adapted to meet the special conditions it faces.

Moreover, the young mammal and, to a rather different extent and in a rather different fashion, the young bird do not simply learn from individual experience. Generally speaking there is also a protective relationship between the parent and the new individual. By example and often by direct intervention the young individual is taught. It heeds and imitates.

As we ascend the scale of cerebral development the possibility of teaching increases. It becomes possible to domesticate and train these higher-brain animals in just the measure that their brains are developed. You can teach very little to a fish or a reptile, but directly you come to the higher cerebral mammals you are confronted by the new possibility of establishing an artificial, taught, motive system to control, supplement or altogether replace natural instinct. You must catch them young. Then you can socialize them and get to quite remarkable working understandings with them. The shepherd's dog, the blind man's dog, the polo pony, the polite, house-trained cat, are examples of the immense individual adaptability which is achieved through the establishment of a taught, secondary self in the cerebral cortex. None of these creatures are behaving in accordance with the primary tendencies they have inherited. They are behaving in accordance with an adaptive mental superstructure imposed upon their natural dispositions. It enables them to survive not simply as tolerated but as contributing individuals in a complex social organization which otherwise would have had no alternative but their extermination. They would have suffered the fate that is overtaking the unteachable Tasmanian Devil or the unteachable Tasmanian Wolf.

## 4

### HISTORY BECOMES ECOLOGY

AT THIS POINT AGAIN it may be well to take stock of the discussion we are unfolding. We have been restating, very plainly and directly, established facts in general ecology, and we are going on now to develop this restatement in relation to the particular position and outlook of the human species. There is no need to apologize for this biological résumé, elementary though it is. It is vitally necessary to our statement. It is absolutely impossible to approach the urgent and distressful problems of the present time with any hope of lucid solution until this general background of knowledge is definitely present in the mind.

From now on we shall encounter an increasing amount and variety of resistance to our application of these almost universally admitted facts. From this point on, many readers will be quite unaccustomed to seeing human social life in the light of ecological science. There is a sort of barrier in their minds. It is not because they do not know, but because they see the two sets of facts apart. They will experience a strong resistance to this invasion of this reserved region of human affairs by these really quite incontrovertible ideas, because in this reserved region their minds are already strongly occupied by idea systems that are incompatible with it....

It has been pointed out how the species of brain-animals co-operate with circumstances in teaching their offspring to adapt themselves to the exactions of their environment. But in the case of man, and to a quite exceptional extent, because of an immense development of speech and gesture, the taught stuff in the cerebrum becomes of overpoweringly greater importance than mere hard experience, and we find the behavior system of the individual molded to social co-operation and collective needs, not only by tradition and other forms of education but by institutions and law. Man, above everything else, is an educated animal, socially controlled. He is no longer primarily or even mainly a creature of instinct and brief individual experience. That phase in evolution lies a million years behind him. His instincts alone and without correction would fail him utterly as a behavior control in his present circumstances.

There is a relatively enormous artificial supplement to the natural man in all of us. We talk of our "selves" and of being freemen, but much the greater part of our activities today we perform as parts *not* of one simple, greater organism, human society, *but,* what is more complex, as parts of a number of greater organisms—profession, township, nation, religion, club, class, and so forth, which are all woven together into what we call human society and our social reactions. What we do as purely spontaneous individuals is hardly more than a narrow choice between prescribed things. The home we live in, the clothes we wear, the food we eat, the way we go about the world, are all substantially imposed upon us by forces exterior to our personalities.

## HISTORY BECOMES ECOLOGY

They are social products and more and more do they become social products.

The socialization of human life, the relative increase of the factor supplied by society, is still going on quite rapidly. There was a time, for instance, not so many generations ago, when most people built their own homes, made their own clothes, got their own food, taught their own children. *Now* the building trade, clothing trade, the provision shop, and the public school see to all that.

This applies with even greater truth to our minds. A mere fraction of our knowledge is self-taught. What we know again is nine-tenths hearsay. We have heard, we have read. The stuff in our heads was mainly put there by society. To the biologist an ordinary ape is just a natural ape, but a man is a natural man *plus* a great cerebral accumulation of directive ideas, prejudices, antagonisms, tolerances and conceptions of what he ought and ought not to do, which wrap about him and fit him into the social body to which he belongs. From the biological point of view all this cerebro-social accumulation of knowledge, beliefs and ideas, responsibilities and dependency, is as much a natural adjustment to needs and environment as a claw or a skull or a swimming bladder; it is a thing of the same kind, though it differs enormously in the relative swiftness and breadth of its adaptability to changing conditions. It is subject to the same ecological laws.

The growth of this mental superstructure upon the primitive ape-man of the later Tertiary period can now be traced in its broad lines without very much difficulty. Any attempt to make a general outline of human history falls almost uncontrollably into the form of a story of developing communication, learning and co-operation between the primordial ape-man family groups. The outline of history as one whole is, and must be, a history of communication and socialization. It is compelled to apprehend primary processes that the older type of history, with its preoccupation with separate communities, was equally compelled to ignore. It begins necessarily with the origins of speech, gesture, drawing, observances, and taboos.

With every such development, the association of human animals in groups collectively more efficient in the appropriation of food supplies became easier. The family group grew into the tribe and tribes grew larger. Their growing awareness of the seasons is apparent in the archæological record; their growing ability to co-operate in the semi-domestication of animals and the first agricultural tentatives is now quite clearly traceable. These are no longer matters to dispute about. With the development of agriculture and the beginnings of settlement, man, the new sort of socialized man, appears as a rapid and immense biological success. His growing communities spread swiftly, growing as well as multiplying and spreading, and displaying every symptom of an unprecedented surplus of biological energy.

A few millenia ago the life which our great-grandfathers considered to be the normal and immemorial life of mankind was well under way. It had grown up, biologically speaking, speaking by the standards of geological time, with the rapidity of a puff-ball, and those who lived it were unaware that there had ever been any other way of human living. Such was life. And it was still, although they did not perceive it in the least, under a stress of accelerating change.

The changes in the conditions of human life during the

last twenty or thirty thousand years have been mainly brought about by the acceleration of invention through increasing co-operation and the release of material and social power. There have been no doubt climatic and geographical changes, but their share has been relatively less important. The essential story of history and pre-history is the story of the adaptation of the social-educated superstructure of the animal man to the novel problems with which his own enterprise and inventiveness have been continually confronting him. Law, religion, education, are from the ecological point of view, names we give to the cardinal aspects of this process of adaptation. Each generation in these growing and spreading societies was told a story of its relation to the community into which it had to fit itself and given an account of the acquiescences and co-operations expected from it. The imperatives of law, education, religion, all flowing into one another and sustaining one another, were expressed, and in these early stages of mental development could only be expressed, by anthropomorphic myths. Natural selection has no care for scientific precision. There is no immediate survival value in truth. To this day the survival value of the critical habit of mind is questionable. It sufficed for the purposes of nature if the myths and the system of observance, the things that were too awful to do and the things that it was fatal to leave undone, made for the survival of the community as a whole. The adaptive superstructures, the laws, rules and beliefs, that were favoring human survival, varied in different regions, but they varied within the limits set by the conditions of specific survival. A certain primary resemblance of the tribal gods and of the tribal stories and of the behavior systems of the differentiating social classes, waited upon the spread of the "normal" way of life about the earth. Parallel circumstances evoked parallel adjustments. Generally the pattern included a tribal ancestor god, a priesthood taking care of the calendar and medicine, a morality of propitiation and self-restraint.

Step by step, as human inter-communication increased, communities grew larger. And as they grew larger they developed something, of which curiously enough we are only beginning to grasp the profound importance today; they developed a superfluity of young men.

From the point of view of the biologist *Homo sapiens* was making an almost excessive success. He was repeating the exuberance of the great Mesozoic reptiles or the early Tertiary deinotheria. The species was not only holding its own, it was spreading and multiplying by leaps and bounds. And the front of its biological advance was this surplus of young men. Young men, full of beans as people say, and looking for trouble.

Hitherto historians have failed to recognize the great importance of this trouble-making stratum. It is well to underline it here. It is a primary social fact. I have been reading recently the works of Mark Benney, *Low Company* and *The Truth about English Prisons* (*Fact,* March 1938), who is rapidly becoming a leading authority on criminology, and he reminds me very strikingly of how nonsensical it is to talk of a criminal class as a different sort of human being. It is in its origins more and more of an age class. Every sort of energetic male human being is a potential criminal, if nothing else is found to occupy and interest him. These expanding human societies in the past were needing less and less energy per head to be sure of their food supply and security. Something had to be done to and for these young men, and the easiest way of keeping them out of mischief, keeping them disciplined in fact and the numbers of them down, was war.

Primitive war was a necessity forced upon the human community by biological success through the production of a surplus of young males. It appeared with herding and agriculture and it was naturally associated with them. In Papua and the Mandated Territory of New Guinea, one can still see humanity in a sort of equilibrium at that stage of development. There you have a population of over half a million, still living in small independent communities, each with its own conceit of itself, its peculiar petty customs and prejudices. These New Guinea peoples are by no means a monotony of barbarism. They present indeed a great variety of physical and mental types, and their social and artistic possibilities are very considerable. Up to the present they have solved their population pressure by spells of not too destructive warfare. There is a little killing-off and then things settle down again. Now, under the parental care of the Canberra government, their warfare is to cease, and what will happen to these peoples is very uncertain. They may be subjected to economic exploitation far more tragic than warfare.

You can write human history in a variety of ways, but one way of writing it would be to consider how, age after age, humanity has met the problem of *What to do with our sons*. There was war and what was generally associated with war, conquest and colonization. Roman Britain, for instance, was conquered by the surplus offspring of the Saxon shore. In my native county, Kent, traces survived until a very recent period of the custom of gavelkind. The elder sons were sent off marauding and the youngest kept the home. You can re-write the history of all the great population movements in terms of the pressure of the young male surplus.

It should be particularly evident as an operating cause in the history of the last two centuries, and it would be if history were properly told. Every community can be shown to be either sending out the plethora of its population as emigrants and settlers, or reducing it by warfare, or else suffering from acute social trouble, such social trouble as the words Russian Hooligans, Chinese Boxers, Moonlighters, Nazis, Fascists, revolutionary terrorists, gangsters, will call to mind. The young man surplus, if it is not consumed, is the main source of rebels, revolutionaries and disturbances of all kinds. Somehow that tension must find relief. The comparative social stability of the nineteenth century was largely due to emigration and the settlement of new lands. Now there are no more new lands open to immigration.

Moreover this tension has been greatly intensified by the huge increase of productive efficiency through invention and the use of mechanical power, which has diminished the number of young men who could look forward to a fairly secure, properly rewarded, sufficiently interesting married life.

Invention and discovery in production have intensified this age-long human problem and contributed to the present exceptional drift towards warfare and social convulsions. People stand in the young man's way and he is ready to get rid of them in any fashion suggested to him. That drift towards a social killing-off, and the necessity of justifying

## HISTORY BECOMES ECOLOGY

it, explain the eagerness with which race difference, class difference, any sort of difference of complexion, language or usage, nationalism and imperialism, are exalted into combatant provocations today. You can waste a lot of time arguing about this or that *ism*. The essential fact is the accumulating tension of unsatisfied youth, and these *isms* are mere formulæ of relief.[1]

Warfare and social conflict have for long ages released the plethoric human species towards the relief of a blood-letting. So it has been through all the ages of recorded history. With the relatively puny means of destruction available before the age of invention and innovation, it was no more than an excretion of inconvenient energy. For some hundreds of centuries humanity got along in this way. War became part of the accepted human rhythm, just as the massacre of the drones is part of the natural rhythm of the honey bee. Laws, customs, morals, sentiments and thoughts were adapted to it so as to make it natural and easy. If it were not for the outbreak of invention and discovery during the past century, man might have gone on drumming and trumpeting his way through long ages yet to come, going to his priest to bless his flags, facing the day of battle bravely, and either dying on the field of honor, or surviving to raise another generation for the same experience.

But that inventive urge in the species has suddenly, in—what is by the geological and biological scales—a mere flash of time, altered all that. It has made war something entirely different and it has put quite a new face on the political ideas, the working conceptions of right and wrong, of duty and service that have hitherto kept the varied and fluctuat-

---

[1] See *Note* 4A. A falling birth-rate does not affect this.

ing patchwork of human communities going. It has strained and distorted the problem of adaptive survival almost beyond recognition. That, concisely, is the clue to the human situation today.

Let me try to give the gist of this vast change. It is a change in human power and scope.

First as to the increase in socially available power. Before the change, except for a little wind power or water power, the only power available for human purposes was a little animal power, horse, ox, elephant, camel, llama, or what not, and man power. The gross total of power units that sufficed to run everything that was going on in Great Britain in a day in the reign of Queen Elizabeth, everything, was probably much less than the total of units that is consumed today in running the lighting and transport alone of such a city as Manchester or Kansas City. And again all the energy of marching, shooting, stabbing, hacking, running to and fro at the battle of Agincourt was probably less than the energy released by one single high explosive shell in a modern bombardment.

Until this change in the total of available power occurred, the great majority of mankind toiled habitually to get food, clothing and shelter. They were under an obligation to do so or want. A small minority contrived in various ways to live by the toil of others and spend, and except for such parasitism there was no way to leisure. Now a steadily dwindling number of people, using power machinery and modern contrivances, can produce the essentials of life in excess of all our requirements. Never before in the history of life has any animal had such a fantastic increase in its ability to make or destroy.

## HISTORY BECOMES ECOLOGY

That is the first aspect of the contemporary change. A second is what is called the abolition of distance. Even more fantastic in relation to past tradition is the increase of speed from point to point. The maximum of speed at which an Elizabethan man could travel was limited by a horse. He could send an uncertain and difficult message a hundred miles a day. He had beacon fires of course, but they do not carry any explicit messages.[1] He could see for a few miles. Now abruptly this creature can travel in comfort three hundred miles an hour, he can see and talk to his fellow-man on the other side of the earth, he can murder him at vast, increasing distances, he knows what is happening all over the world almost instantaneously. And his health improves and his vitality is greater. On the average he lives almost twice as long and twenty times as actively and variously as his great-great-grandfather. Now that distance has been abolished, he lives with increasing restlessness cheek by jowl with all the rest of mankind. So far a biologist might count him an unqualified success in the struggle for life—except for one disconcerting thing. He is ceasing to breed. His numbers are now passing a maximum and seem fated to decline, at least for some decades ahead. Woman for a variety of reasons is betraying an increasing disinclination to bear children. Man's conquest of nature may prove a sterile conquest.

His reproduction is falling off and his behavior traditions and controls, and more particularly the war tradition, are producing the most devastating tragedies among his communities. The effect of the increase of power has been to exaggerate the impact of the war drive monstrously. One

[1] See *Note* 4B.

may compare the human species today to a steamship that has long sailed the seas with engines roughly adequate to its needs, until some malign influence has suddenly gone down into the engine-room and, without any consultation with the ship's officers, amplified the power of the engines a thousandfold. Now they are flying loose out of control, lashing the ship to pieces, and threatening to sink it altogether. The captain upon the bridge gives impotent orders; the engineers dodge the pounding shafts and the escaping, searching, scalding steam.

Because of the way in which science and invention have brought us all into intimate contact and put high explosives into our hands, war has become a process of destruction that spares neither age nor sex, it is no longer a selective elimination of the surplus young men, it is a colossal wastage of material resources, a rapid disintegration of the social organization, robbed of all the glories and gallantries that once adorned it. In the past it was a corrective and almost tonic process. Now it has become a rapid wasting disease, a galloping consumption of the human species.

## 5

## UNION NOW?

IS IT POSSIBLE FOR man to recover control, or is this shattering return to destructive violence the beginning of the end of the career of *Homo sapiens*? Let us hold firmly to the broad conceptions of ecological science that have brought us thus far. The human species is, as a whole, dangerously out of harmony with these new conditions. Either its powers of adaptation will be sufficient to readjust it to the new demands, and it will go on to a new phase of survival, or, like any other living species, it will be defeated, shattered and ultimately wiped out. There are no other possibilities.

There is no time for any of the slower and more ancient methods of adaptation. The readjustment needed must be a mental readjustment. In that alone is there any hope for mankind.

In view of what has gone before it is plain that that mental readjustment must involve three main essentials. In varying measure these essentials are already widely recognized.

First and most obviously the idea and tradition of war must be eliminated. For that, quite a large number of people seem to be more or less prepared. They desire it, even if they have yet to discover the price that must be paid for it. Secondly, and what is not nearly so widely conceded, the vast and violent wastage of natural resources in the hunt for private profit that went on during the nineteenth century, must be arrested and reversed by the establishment of a collective economy for the whole world. And thirdly, in view of the stress of those young people, the resultant world organization must be of an active, progressive, imaginatively exciting nature. That surplus energy of youth, male and female, must be used up. It is the drive and essence of life; it is life itself. It must in each generation be "getting on." It must be doing things, making or re-making with an effect of conquest and general participation. The earlier years were preparation; the later, relieved of the high fever and impatience of that full onset of vitality, are appreciation, deliberation and the continual broadening-out of the human agenda.

These three propositions, peace, collectivism and incessant new enterprise, are interdependent and practically inseparable. One cannot be realized without the other two. In stating these propositions we are not in any way "laying down the law." The law is in the nature of things. We are merely stating as precisely as possible the unconditional terms that our race manifestly has to expect.

To what extent is contemporary thought and education moving towards the abolition of war?

An increasing number of us are realizing that the age of independent sovereign states and empires throughout the world, free to make war and prepared to make war, each separated from the other by barriers of language, religion, historical delusions and those differences in habits of life which are called national cultures, is coming to an end, obviously, rapidly; and at present not one of us can say with any confidence what sort of world order can replace it. A world order we feel there must be, but as to how it is to be attained, we are all at sixes and sevens.

The world of man has to become, has—in a chaotic disorder of conflict—already become, one community—one disorderly community. In the days of Oliver Goldsmith, what happened in China, happened in China, and did not matter a rap to anyone in England. If every time one fired a gun in England, he remarked, a man died in China, nobody would mind in the least. The shooting would go on. Now what happens in China, happens everywhere in the world; that is to say it is known and affects life everywhere. The crude fact of the world-wide community is here now. The open questions arise when we consider *how* this inevitable coming together of our communities can and will be recognized and established as a world order.

We have indeed already seen one attempt to reconstitute human affairs so as to eliminate this destructive process of modern war, in the League of Nations experiment. That, we realize now, was an extremely naive attempt to stop the current of history and to preserve forever just those national separatisms and strangulating boundaries against which the stars in their courses are fighting. Certain minimum changes were to be made to "end war" while everything else was to go on just as it had been going on before. Sovereign states, organized essentially for defense and aggression, were to form a League to end combat. Simply that. The conception of an organized World Pax, after it had played its part in the warfare of propaganda, after it had been used to build up false expectations of a new start in life for the German people, was taken over at Versailles and translated into the ideology of Foreign Offices and the diplomatic services. These essential organs of the old regime were instructed to supersede themselves and they were left to work out the task, and quite naturally they did nothing of the sort. The League Covenant completely disregarded that perennial problem of the restless young men, and it gave no attention to the absolute necessity of reconstructing economic life upon a collective basis throughout the world. These are matters about which diplomacy has never concerned itself. They do not enter into diplomatic or political education, which is at least the better part of a century out of date.

At the end of less than a score of years the failure of the League of Nations experiment is complete, and we will spend no time on enlarging upon that fruitless interlude of half-hearted idealism. Suffice it to say that for many excellent minds it has blocked the way to a realistic treatment of the human problem for two decades. We find now in 1939, a rough reproduction of the world situation of 1914-18. We find three aggressive military states threatening the whole world, and we find a number of threatened states contemplating some sort of loosely organized resistance to that aggression.

How loosely—with what dangerous looseness—that organization is still contemplated is illustrated by a book that has recently been given quite serious attention in Britain and America. This is *Union Now* by Clarence K. Streit. He proposes that right now there shall be a "federal" union of fifteen now independent states which he describes as democracies. They are the United States of America, the British group, Finland, France, Holland, Belgium, Switzerland, Denmark, Norway, Sweden. It is not a League or a war alliance he proposes but a permanent federation on the American model, with a common foreign policy, common money, common armed forces, common control of interstate and foreign trade and a common citizenship. He sweeps aside such questions as the status of India, colonial possessions, the various monarchist traditions involved, as secondary questions. Soviet Russia he balances on the brim of his project with a query—on the whole an encouraging query. Apparently the federated democracies are to have great local economic autonomy within the limits of the federal constitution.

Before we look into Mr. Streit's proposals more closely, it will be worth while to get this loose word "democracy" defined. The special interest of his book here lies in the fact that it has been well received by a considerable number of considerable people. It is an intimation of how rapidly opinion is moving towards the conception of a new world order transcending existing boundaries. So far it is a book to be welcomed. But it is also an indication of the extreme vagueness still prevalent about the necessary material and mental conditions of such a world order. Its pseudo-practical short-sightedness is almost as manifest as the boldness of its intention.

I do not believe that a world order can come into existence without a preliminary mental cosmopolis. I may be mistaken in that. Political federation, loose and confused at first, may precede and impose the necessary mental adaptations. That is too round-about and slow a process for the limitations of my imagination. World democracy, I believe, would get lost on the way.

# 6

## WHAT IS DEMOCRACY?

SINCE AT ANY TIME now we may find ourselves fighting, enduring and dying for "democracy," it seems worth while to ask for some clear definition of what democracy means, so that we shall not only fight for it, but be prepared to see that in the end we get it. When you question people closely in the matter, you will encounter a considerable variety of answers, but you will find as you sort them out and arrange them that they do tend to converge and point in a common direction. There is a vital intention beneath the endless misuses and perversions of the word.

Towards what do these diverse statements converge? What is the reality, implicit and potential, that gives its living, present appeal to the word *democracy*?

Two words that will come out very frequently in the definitions that are given you are "freedom" and "liberty." Frequent, but not quite so frequent, are such phrases as the "right" of individuals and communities to "self-government." A few people will make a vote the symbol of democracy. But all of them can be brought into agreement that democracy means the subordination of the state to the ends and welfare of the common individual. Very prevalent is an attitude of negation. Democracy, it is declared, is an

## WHAT IS DEMOCRACY?

*anti*-movement. It demands the protection of the individual life from the state. It is anti-Fascist, anti-Nazi, anti-Communist, anti-war—since there is no liberty in a state of siege—it is the denial of the right of the state organization to interfere in the life of the common individual except for the common convenience and with the common consent.

All this is matter of general agreement, but in all these phrases, there is an element of idealistic overstatement, and as soon as we attempt to bring them into effective contact with the realities of life, we find ourselves involved in some of the standing controversies that have exercised humanity since human thought and discussion began. We are reminded that there is no such thing as absolute freedom or absolute servitude. Limitless freedom, anarchy, would be a world of chaotic conduct, ruled only by impulse, a jungle life. All freedom in any society is conditional; it is a compromise; it implies "rules of the game," that is to say, law. Behind all actual social behavior there is the suggestion of a defined give-and-take, a "social contract." The social contract may vary between the extremes of a contract of blind obedience on the one hand and a contract to undertake no collective action whatever without a plebiscite, an entirely impracticable subordination of the law to mass impulse, on the other. Between these extremes and with a declared bias for conscious, free, individual action whenever it is practicable, this *democracy* falls.

Now the desire for conscious, free, individual action is innate in the normal human being. But it can be inhibited by fear of known or unknown consequences, by indolence and following the drift, and by a complex of infantile dispositions to imitate and obey. The herd instinct is very strong in the immature human animal. It will follow a leader or stampede like a cow, and find great relief from perplexity in doing so. The preference of democracy for the practical maximum of conscious, free, individual action requires a justification beyond the mere faltering desire in our hearts to "stand up, look heaven in the face and be a man."

For the normal man, unrestrained democracy is a very exacting way of living indeed. It asks too much of his natural resources. In a thousand situations even a wise or able man may find himself unable to decide upon the line of action that is fairly the best for himself and also the best for the general good, and in ten thousand he will find a fatal delay in his decisions. For that reason, a detailed, comprehensive, agreed-upon, accessible and understandable system of laws, which are really rules for behavior in predigested situations, is a necessary preliminary condition for a modern democracy. A taxi-cab tariff or the rule of the road or a minimum wage is a convenient elementary instance of the way in which conscious, free, individual action is set aside to the general benefit in a modern, democratic community. We extend that principle nowadays to rates of interest and inordinate profits, to the acquisition of land and many forms of property and to an increasing number of ordinary transactions. Our modern democratic community would frustrate its own declared aims without a complete, detailed, legal framework enforced by a judiciary and a police acting strictly under the law. The man who in a breath will say "I am a democrat" and also "I am a rebel" is simply a fool.

The contrast between democracy and the forms of community with which it is generally contrasted lies essentially in this reliance upon law. In a democracy a man does or should know, or should be easily able to ascertain, exactly "where he stands," what he must do, what he may do, what cannot be done, and he should be able to say with the utmost confidence, "You be damned" to any illegal order or request. The laws that restrain and protect him have received his implicit or expressed consent, and he has a reasonable right to attempt to alter them if he finds them uncongenial, but until they are altered they must be respected by all, small or great, in the community. The President or ruling assembly is as much bound by the law as the meanest citizen.

On the other hand the dictatorships and undemocratic social organizations generally, subject a large part of the common man's activities to uncovenanted restrictions, interference and compulsion. It is plainly contrary to the spirit of democracy that a man should sell himself into slavery or bind himself indefinitely to unquestioning obedience. The care of democracy for freedom extends to the protection of a man from his own desperate necessity. No democracy would tolerate Esau's bargain. Most existing dictatorships, indeed, claim a sort of legality based upon some forced plebiscite, some snatched election. But your inquiries will make it plain that the consent of the governed in a democracy can never be a finally silenced and irrevocable consent. It must be a continuing consent. It must be subject to sustained revision and renewal. From the point of view of democracy all absolutisms are illegal, and resistance to their commands is as justifiable as resistance to any less general hold-up or act of violence.

This fundamental legalism of democracy has been and

is a deterrent to swift collective action, and the history of human government is very largely a history of attempts to reconcile the bickering gradualism of legal and deliberative government under democratic conditions with the needs of special emergencies. Before flood, fire, pestilence, earthquake, war, and especially in war, men have had to relinquish their liberty of individual action more or less completely to a higher command of some sort with unqualified immediate powers. The original "dictators" of the Roman system were essentially legal officials, and one of the primary riddles of human society has been the resumption of power by the community at the end of a period of crisis. A democracy needs to be in a state of perpetual vigilance against the specialist. From Cæsar to Stalin, democracy has been trapped into one-man tyrannies by crises.

But historical analogies are always misleading, and modern crises become more and more elaborate affairs and less and less controllable by single individuals. None of these modern dictatorships has yet been tried out in a sustained war. It is at least highly doubtful whether the vast communities of today, if they are able to develop a class of competent public servants, with a co-operative morale and a sense of public criticism, may not attain an efficiency and a toughness far beyond that of a system subjected to the freaks and inspirations of a single individual. But they must work in the light. They must work with the distinctive freedom and the conscious individual co-operation of a team of football players, and they must be subjected to the continual criticism of an understanding public opinion with unlimited freedom of expression and with an ultimate, if deferred, right of intervention.

## WHAT IS DEMOCRACY?

This conception of the superior flexibility and efficiency of free teamwork, as against dictatorially planned work, is very attractive to the democratically-minded, but it may easily be exaggerated. For example, Tom Wintringham in his *English Captain* lays great stress on the technical superiority of free men, inspired by a common idea, over the conscript soldiers of a dictatorship. He was in the fortunate position of leading a battalion of English volunteers, exceptionally intelligent and enthusiastic, picked men who wanted to fight, who were keen to fight, and unanimous at least in their hostility to the Franco pronunciamento. Of such individuals, unanimous for the services that engage them, an enlightened democracy should no doubt consist. But when one turns to the story Major José Martín Blásquez tells in *I Helped to Build an Army*, of the internal struggles and indiscipline of the defenders of the Republic, one realizes that practical freedom of initiative may achieve the most disastrous confusion.

There is indeed no guarantee of either immediate or ultimate victory in democracy. On that we must insist. There is no inherent magic successfulness in democratic freedom. Democratic freedom may be much more vulnerable than slavery, less easy both to attain and maintain. It may be that few or none of us realize yet the full price that may have to be paid for it.

None the less it is only through the attainment of a real world democracy that there is any hope for the ultimate survival of our species.

In many of the replies one will receive to the demand for a clear definition of democracy, one will get some reference to that magnificent outbreak of the common sense of mankind, the first French Revolution. That remains still a cardinal event in the history of human liberation. It was not the beginning of liberation but it was its most outstanding assertion. The democracy of America, the radicalism of Britain in its most vigorous phase, derived plainly from that French initiative. And since in those days titles and privileges were the most conspicuous infringements of men's liberties, democracy from the outset would have none of them; it was equalitarian without qualification. It was republican, it denied and repudiated any form of class rule whatever—and whenever it is still in health it remains republican and equalitarian.

But conditions in eighteenth-century France were peculiar in the fact that then the conspicuous offense against human liberty was class privilege. For many people in those days the possession of private property was a means of independence, freedom of ownership seemed a reasonable provision for democratic liberty, and only a few realized that, released from class tyranny, the free play of proprietorship might create advantages and disadvantages as wide and socially wasteful, as subject to "abuses," as the class privileges of the older regime. Throughout the first revolutionary period the spirit of democracy found itself puzzled, mocked and frustrated by economic inequality. Men freed from the tyranny of privileges found themselves oppressed by a tyranny of advantages. The common man, theoretically free and independent, discovered himself in the grip of an expanding economic system that made free competitive employment only another form—and to many it seems a scarcely preferable form—of serfdom. Political equality by itself proved in practice to be no equality at all.

## WHAT IS DEMOCRACY?

Accordingly when we pursue our inquiries into the meaning of democracy today, we find a definite cleavage from this point onward in the replies to the question of "What is democracy?" An increasing number will be forced to agree that collective economic controls, "Industrial Democracy," as Beatrice Webb first phrased it very happily, in her study of co-operation (1891), constitute a necessary completion of the democratic proposition. A dwindling minority clings to the private profit system as the logical method of the sturdy individualism of the revolution. But the general implication of modern democracy is that unrestrained economic advantage can be an even graver infringement of human liberty than privilege. Modern democracy is not only legalism and equalitarianism; it is socialism. It sets its face against all abuse of the advantages of ownership.

Democracy is socialism, and also, by a natural extension of its equalitarianism as the problem of world law becomes urgent, it is cosmopolitan. Almost tacitly democracy has accepted and assimilated the necessity that law must be world law and equally protective of every individual human being.

So far as cosmopolitanism goes, modern democracy reverts to far older revolts of human common sense against racial, national and class distinctions. Since the rise of Buddhism there has been hardly any broad religious initiative that has not at least paid lip service to this idea which, in Christianity for example, is incorporated in the formula of an impartial divine fatherhood and an equal brotherhood of man. In *The Outline of History* the association of cosmopolitanism with theocrasia and the appearance of the syncretic universal religions is traced. There was a double impulse from below and from above; the desire of the expanding empires to fuse local particularisms into a larger order under the God-Emperor was in accordance with the craving of normal common sense to escape from the irksomeness of obviously artificial estrangements. Dr. T. J. Haarhoff, quoting W. W. Tarn's *Alexander and the Unity of Mankind,* declares that Alexander "was the pioneer of one of the supreme revolutions in the world outlook, the first man known to us who contemplated the brotherhood of man or the unity of mankind." This is an exaggeration of a significant fact. Cosmopolitanism, universal brotherhood, has indeed been appearing and reappearing in human thought for at least the past four and twenty centuries, like sunshine trying to break through a cloudy sky.

Now the "democracy" that found its expression in the first French Revolution, the American Revolution and the liberal movement throughout the world, was not only incomplete upon the economic side and had, later and with difficulty, to become socialist in order to preserve its liberating intention, but also it was very sketchy and indefinite in the matter of education.

This was due to the fact that the ideology of the Great Revolution was essentially middle-class in its origins. It sprang from a social stratum already educated and so satisfied with the sufficiency of its general education and so accustomed to a supply of books and pamphlets, that it did not realize that there was anything exceptional in the knowledge and freedom of thought it enjoyed. It did not even apprehend its immense and immediate obligations to the Encyclopædists in organizing its ideas. It took their contribution for granted. It launched its generous proposition of

## WHAT IS DEMOCRACY?

universal equality indeed, but not only did it fail to realize the need to insure freedom from economic pressure, but also it neglected to organize the education of the community as one whole. The American Revolution, in this respect, with, for example, its provision of State universities, seems to have been ahead of the French. Nevertheless it took the better part of a century for democracy to realize, even to a limited extent, the third vital implication of its demand for liberty, equality, and fraternity, which was the free and necessary universal education of the democratic community to a common level of understanding and co-operation. Communities in which every mentally normal citizen can at least read and write, have existed for less than a century. Communities in which the common education rises much above that level do not yet exist.

That freedom and equality are incomplete without freely accessible knowledge and free and open discussion is a necessary completion of the democratic idea, but it is one upon which the inquirer into the meaning of democracy will get the least assurance. If he asks leading questions, he will get a general admission that universal education and sound, ample information upon every matter of collective concern are necessary elements in the democratic proposition, but unless he himself introduces the matter he will hear very little insistence upon this vital completion of the democratic ideal.

He will indeed encounter a certain amount of impatience if he stresses this matter. Ordinary people resent being told that they are undereducated or wrongly educated. To the common man and woman today, prepared though their minds seem to be now for a socialist cosmopolis of a quite generous type, education still means just any old education, and news is what a press run entirely for profit and political and social ends, and (in the British system) a government-controlled radio, choose to tell them. It is the education they have grown up to, and so far they have not been awakened to its insufficiency. They want to carry out these new conceptions of life at that level. To raise that level seems to them irksome and uncalled for.[1]

It is still possible therefore for the equalitarian impulse to be effectively frustrated in practice by deliberate and systematic miseducation and misinformation. The common man and woman know now in general terms and pretty definitely what they want, but they still do not know how to state and demand what they want. Private enterprise is able to defend its appropriations quite effectively, because it owns the press almost entirely, the news agencies and the distributing trades, and so it can distort values and distract the public from crucial issues in the boldest fashion. There is no countervailing equipment of the public mind in the common schools. These are essentially conservative institutions, adapting the common man to the social order in which he finds himself, preparing him for that state of life to which he has been called, and giving him no reasonable intimations of the great drama of change in which he has to play his part. As we have shown, the whole mechanism of modern life demands organized collective control. The stars in their courses will not suffer the world scramble of exploitation that wasted so much human possibility in the nineteenth century to go on. Our species cannot afford it

[1] See *Note* 6A.

under any conditions. But in face of the essential ignorance of the modern "democratic" community, the enterprising owner, the profiteer that is to say, can keep his grip upon his advantages far more effectively than he can in the face of a dictator with unqualified powers. He can resist socialization far more effectively.

Against the capitalist's obstructive power the willfulness of the dictator is able to operate far more vigorously than the will of the under-educated, ill-informed and suggestible "democracies." So that in certain ways the dictatorships have undoubtedly been able to get ahead of the "democratic" states. They have gone further on the way to socialization. While the industrial exploiter or the rich man struggles to keep his grip on the recalcitrant worker below, the dictator of the totalitarian state takes him firmly by the collar. Wealth finds itself handled with an extraordinary disrespect. Dictatorships imply collectivism. They are forced to collectivism in the face of bargaining wealth and the uneasy claims of their own supporters. They are forced towards a comprehensive efficiency. The only effective response to totalitarian collectivism on the part of a freedom-seeking community is a scientifically planned and directed socialism.

From the economic point of view, the whole difference now between the reality of dictatorship and the ideal of democracy, when it is worked out to its practical completion, is the difference between socialization in the dark, with all the progressive corruption, appropriation and inefficiency that spring up in the dark, and socialization in the light of an alert and implemented public opinion; between socialization by compulsion or socialization by enlightened consent.

From the point of view of the individual the difference is one between a deadening servitude and a continual participating enlargement of responsible life. No existing institutions coming to us from the past can represent democracy as it is thus conceived; it is a far bolder thrust towards a new order than any of these adventurer systems that stand in its path.

If now we fill in the gaps in the current conception of democracy by insisting upon complete educational equalitarianism, if we dot the *i*'s and cross the *t*'s that are still undotted and uncrossed, if we transcend any accepted contemporary rendering of the idea, then "democracy" does indeed become a very magnificent conception of a new life for man.

If democracy means economic justice and the attainment of that universal sufficiency that science assures us is possible today; if democracy means the intensest possible fullness of knowledge for everyone who desires to know and the greatest possible freedom of criticism and individual self-expression for anyone who desires to object; if democracy means a community saturated with the conception of a common social objective and with an educated will like the will of a team of football players to co-operate willingly and understandingly upon that objective; if democracy means a complete and unified police control throughout the world, to repress the financial scramble and gangster violence which constitute the closing phase of the sovereign state and private ownership system; then we have in democracy a conception of life for which every intelligent man and woman on earth may well be prepared to live, fight or die, as circumstances may require.

But that rounded-off and completed realization of democracy is still only establishing itself against great resistances in the human mind. It is not as yet established there. And still less is it established as the guiding faith of any political or social organization whatever.

# 7

## WHERE IS DEMOCRACY?

WHERE IN ALL THIS collection of governments Mr. Streit would have us federate, is there one that satisfies this plain bare statement of the growing and deepening significance of the democratic idea?

France depends for its mental expression upon an alliance of reactionary papers and for its foreign policy upon an association of diplomatists and army chiefs, which has held together throughout its dynastic and political fluctuations in one consistent policy for the security and advancement of *La France*. America tempers a wide tolerance of free speech and personal criticism with a press-sustained persecution of labor leaders, radicals, "reds" and "agitators" generally. Its press, if less centralized than the French and so less concerted, is equally commercial. The freedom of expression of its university professors is pinched between the possibility of dismissal for excessive outspokenness from above and the attacks of the press-man from below. The American record of successfully framed-up cases against troublesome workers' leaders is a long and discreditable one, and one need only glance reproachfully at the distressful history of color prejudice, unincorporated townships and the exploitation of penal labor in the more backward states. And yet these two are the "democracies" *par excellence.*

Most of the European states invited to Mr. Streit's federation are not even democratic in profession. Sweden, Norway, Denmark, Holland and the British Empire are monarchies; the monarch professes to act only on the advice of his or her ministers, but as a matter of fact the court is a center of social and administrative influence of an entirely undemocratic sort. A crown is the symbol of graded privilege. In the place of *Heil Hitler* or the Fascist salute, these royalist peoples, at the sound of their particular Royal Anthem, stand stiffly to attention with an air of ineffable reverence. It is a quite parallel act of worship, and as complete a repudiation of the personal responsibility of democracy.

The disintegrating British Empire is now, one has to recognize, a system of government almost completely out of popular control. Practically it has undergone a reactionary revolution in the last decade, and a loose-knit combination of court, church, army and wealth, intensely class-conscious, intensely self-protective, has resumed control of affairs. It is an oligarchy skillful in the assimilation of useful or formidable individuals but without the slightest disposition to amalgamate with anything else on earth. Its ruling motive is the fear of dispossession. Decisions involving peace or war are made without any pretense of consulting any surviving popular will, and the whole capitalist press, the cinema, the radio and indeed all possible means of influencing opinion, concentrate upon the assertion of the rightness and inevitableness of these decisions. Dissent is a muffled and ineffective squeaking, and any inconvenient facts are kept from the public by requests for suppression that are in effect commands. There is a special Form D sent round to the press which it is extremely unwise to defy. Most of the acts of Mr. Chamberlain since September 1938 have been as irresponsible as those of any Dictator, equally unscrupulous and far more shameful. He has indeed made himself a Dictator by tact and betrayal instead of by violent seizure. There is in the long run very little to choose between a bully dictatorship and a "tact" dictatorship. The latter may be less crushing but more insidious in its attack upon human dignity.

These are the practical realities Mr. Streit has to face. The will for federation in any of these governments is more than doubtful—even if presently they have their backs to the wall. They will all fight for their separate sovereignty to the last.

No doubt it is true that, in spite of much human inconsistency, much confused thinking and many local abuses, there is still a powerful disposition throughout all the Atlantic and Scandinavian communities towards liberty, equality and world brotherhood. It breaks out in literature, discussion and conduct. It expresses itself plainly in books, spontaneous press writing, plays and films. This is most manifest in America and there is in consequence a growing disposition of the British authorities to intercept and censor the too outspoken American weekly press. An increasing number of English readers subscribe to American periodicals to learn what is being hushed up in their own country.

With every acceleration of communications this American influence will increase. Moreover, there are plenty of American professors manifestly disposed to take the risk of outspokenness and say what they like. If at times they veil their meaning a little from the possible hostility of the unintelligent in a deliberate obscurity of technicality that sometimes borders on jargon, that does not prevent their speculating very boldly about economic, social and international processes, much more boldly and freshly than their English equivalents.

Again the bitter jests of such a French periodical as *Le Canard Enchâiné* are saturated with the soundest democratic scorn and derision. The desire of a considerable section of enlightened Frenchmen to sustain and complete the mighty impetus of the Declaration of the Rights of Man is genuine and obstinate. They will not willingly suffer France to desist from her traditional task of world enlightenment. For some years, in the face of overwhelming financial and political difficulties, there has been a gallant attempt to produce a modern encyclopædia, which might repeat the preparatory role of the original Encyclopædists for the vaster needs of today.[1] Neither Americans nor British, with their vastly greater resources, have attempted anything so comprehensive and illuminating. It would be possible to quote hundreds of instances, names, books, speeches, utterances and acts, to show that all round and about the world in a great multitude of still all-too-dispersed intelligences, democracy lives and advances.

But these evidences of a considerable and growing will for a reasonably complete democracy do not alter the fact that the directive forces in control of this miscellany of states Mr. Streit and his disciples would have us federate, are scarcely more democratic in structure and method than those running the frankly anti-democratic states.

[1] See *Note* 7A, the Italian *Encyclopædia*.

Indeed, to call the present world convulsion a war between the "allied democracies" of the world and "totalitarian states," is putting all too fine a name upon it. The reality will be a war of established governments and governing systems claiming to represent "democracy" but quite unwilling and unprepared to set themselves to realize the modern democratic idea, against expansive desperado governments that have shown themselves contemptuous of democratic pretensions and dangerous to the general peace. It will be another war for the alteration or preservation of frontiers.

It is almost impossible to hope that this complex of warfare towards which the world is drifting can assume any other form than a confused alliance against these more lawless military powers, whatever formal victories or defeats ensue. It is incredible that there will not be a steady deterioration in human morale through the stresses of the struggle. If the so-called aggressor states are defeated, their unfortunate common people will be saddled with the war guilt of the governments that have enslaved and ruined them. They will be made to "pay" again. Another insincere attempt to organize "collective security" on the lines of the League of Nations, another unstable League of victors, will simply accumulate the necessary resentments for another collapse into still more violent conflict. Fresh brigand adventurers will appear, trading on the shame and despair of the vanquished.

It is this that makes the approach of this second world-war storm so black. Whichever side emerges at any particular phase as victorious, is really a secondary issue. The practical loss of freedom, the usurpation of controls, seems inevitable.

## WHERE IS DEMOCRACY? 63

The possibility of an emergence of any sort of enhancement of democracy from the threatened *mêlée* seems very slight indeed. Democracy is still too incomplete, unorganized and unprepared to bring about any such happy ending. Catastrophe is still steadily outrunning education. We are at present rapidly experiencing a repetition of 1914-1919 on a vastly more disastrous scale.

# 8

## WHAT MAN HAS TO LEARN

If we hold firmly to that same systematic assembling of universally acceptable statements which has brought us thus far, it is not overwhelmingly difficult to state the nature of the mental adaptation that is needed to arrest this present drive towards biological disaster for *Homo sapiens*. If it has become necessary for him to be re-educated as a conscious world citizen, to be prepared to take his place in a collective world fellowship, then plainly the realization of this necessity is the framework upon which his social being must be rebuilt. The scientific vision of life in the universe and no other has to be his vision of the universe. Any other leads ultimately to disaster. And since the existing educational organization of the world does not provide anything like that vision nor establish the necessary conceptions of right conduct that arise out of it, it needs to be recast quite as much and even more than the political framework needs to be recast. This may involve, it will almost certainly involve, such a *Kulturkampf* as the world has never seen before. But since it is the only possible line of survival, that effort has to be faced. Unless there is sufficient mental and moral vigor in our race to achieve the educational readjustment, then there seems to be nothing that can possibly arrest the present *dégringolade* of *Homo sapiens*.

## 9

### SAMPLE OF A GENERATION

Let us be as full and explicit as possible about this reorganization of man's mental superstructure, this reconditioning of his apparatus for adaptation, that we are stressing.

And here again there is nothing original and hardly anything that is fairly controversial in what will be stated here. The only originality lies in an adherence to one consistent line of thought, to carrying the broad and practically indisputable statements of modern ecological science, unimpaired, into the field of current human affairs and refusing to be deflected or complicated by secondary and irrelevant considerations.

It happens to have been my role throughout life to assemble facts and interpretations of fact, bearing upon man's power of controlling his future. From the days of that paradoxical fantasy, *The Time Machine* (1894) onward, my mind, partly no doubt by the accidents of life, but partly also, I think, by a natural predisposition, has been directed more and more definitely to the question of what is likely to happen in the future. And looking back upon this half-century of discussion and suggestion and tracing its development phase by phase, a very remarkable change in the whole tenor of human thought becomes manifest.

It is only now, indeed, as I bring all these things together to review, that I realize how our attitude to past and future has changed since the later-Victorian period. There has been an almost complete reorientation, at once profound and subtle, of our minds with regard to time.

Briefly: the intelligence of the nineties attached much more importance to the past and much less to the probabilities of the days to come, than do any contemporary minds now. It was living in what appears now as an almost static present. The past supplied a picturesque system of justifications for the established state of affairs, but it was the established state of affairs alone which had any quality of reality. There was a widespread feeling that nothing more of primary importance was ever likely to happen. Life as we knew it was a leisurely game of consequences. It is difficult now, even for those of us who were already living in those days, to recall the entire absence of *urgency* that prevailed. We were carried along by habit and that false sense of security which the absence of fundamental crises engenders. To most of my generation in the eighties and nineties, all the cardinal discoveries of science seemed to have been made, all the great political systems established for good, the world permanently apportioned among the Powers. We had a sort of feeling that Queen Victoria, under whose rule everybody up to high middle age had been born, would go on living forever. The future was something in another universe, in another dimension. One could say or think anything one liked about it because it did not seem to matter in the least.

This habit of mind lingered long after the beliefs on which it had been established had decayed. It lingers still.

One factor in the steadily accelerated swing from traditionalism and legalism to futurism, that presently began, was certainly the enlargement of our horizons by the realization of evolution and geological time and the breaking of the barriers set to our imaginations by the myth of the Creation and the Fall. But at first there was—how can one put it?—an intellectual but not a practical release. It was still possible in *The Time Machine* to imagine humanity on the verge of extinction and differentiated into two decadent species, the Eloi and the Morlocks, without the slightest reflection upon everyday life. Quite a lot of people thought that idea was very clever in its sphere, very clever indeed, and no one minded in the least. It seemed to have no sort of relation whatever to normal existence.

To a large extent, I shared that detachment. If I was imaginatively futurist, I was for all practical purposes contemporaneous. The possible extinction of humanity appeared to be something so remote that it never gave me a moment's real uneasiness in those days. The future was still no more real than dreamland.

But all that has changed, and I have come through the phases of that change. Now the questions: "What is going to happen?" and "And then what will happen?" dominate an increasing number of awakening minds among which I am moving. We live in a planning world. Everything we do is becoming preparatory and anticipatory. Today has vanished almost completely in our enormous preoccupation with tomorrow.

I suppose I have responded as much as anyone in my generation to this mental rotation. There is no need therefore for me to apologize for using myself as the trace of the flow of thought during the past half century. I happen to be the most convenient trace. If I were not so, then somebody else should be writing this book instead of me.

To begin with I used the future as a field for purely imaginative play. After *The Time Machine* I wrote some more futuristic stories. But as one followed another I found I was less and less interested in the artistic business of making the tale plausible and more and more in the scientific interest of making it probable. The turn of the century set many of us forecasting in earnest. My natural bias or my journalistic instinct, or maybe both in unison, moved me to write *Anticipations* (1900), in which I threw the teller of fantastic tales aside altogether and set myself speculating about the coming years. I was moving with the times. The book caught on; it was more successful than most novels; it was one of the first of such books to sell well. I will not say anything of its guesses, some happy, some wildly out. But it left me with the persuasion that here was something needing to be done and which could be done much more thoroughly than I had done it. My sense of the importance and reality of the future increased.

In 1902 I was reading a paper to the Royal Institution, *The Discovery of the Future,* in which I was boldly asserting the need to realize and accept a forward-looking system of values. I presently found myself in correspondence with various parallel groups abroad which, half in defiance and half in burlesque, were proclaiming the Futurist doctrine. Among them was Signor Marinetti, who came to London reciting, in a tremendous voice, the most astounding Futurist poetry. He resented with extreme bitterness the English and American tourists in Italy with their red guide-books

## SAMPLE OF A GENERATION

like catalogues at a sale. He was, he said, prepared to destroy all the historical monuments in the peninsula. He demanded, loudly and violently, a living country and not a museum of antiques.

The impulse spread, but still for a great number even of progressive-minded people it retained a quality of unreality. It was an exuberance for them, a lark, a fashion. This Futurist stuff, they felt, could not last. In practice they still clung to the established order for their permanent values. It was the shock and stresses of the Great War that wrenched them away finally from this assumption of permanent stability towards a reluctant, imperfect recognition of the greater importance of the anticipatory aspect of life. It was like the internal change-over that must happen in a bar of iron when it is magnetized. And many quite intelligent people were not wrenched away. They kept up their resistances, and a large body of the educated still resist—as we shall see. But the forward-looking section accumulated conviction; their sense of reality continued to shift away more and more decisively from the thing that is to the thing that is to be. *The Discovery of the Future* became by degrees a matter-of-fact statement for me instead of a daring thesis. I believed in it as time went on much more than I had done when first I launched it.

As the war unfolded before me, my mind was increasingly obsessed by the problem of how the war would end and what would come after the war. Imaginative people were guessing and inferring and making plans. The word "plan" became more and more frequent; at length no newspaper was complete without it. A Ministry of Foresight was suggested. We busied ourselves in making the New Map of

Europe, the New Map of the World. The idea of a "League of Nations" emerged amidst this ferment of anticipatory projects. An interesting phase in all this forward-looking peering was the War Aims controversy. I happened to be working in Northcliffe's Ministry of Propaganda in Enemy Countries.[1] I was in particular directing the propaganda in Germany, and, in co-operation with Dr. J. W. Headlam-Morley, I induced our Crewe House colleagues to draw up a memorandum upon the allied war aims and submit it to the Foreign Office for endorsement. "This," we said, "is what we suppose we are fighting for, and if we can get this we shall be satisfied and the war will be at an end. Is that so? We cannot go on with our work properly unless we know its objective." The War Office was profoundly shocked. Whatever else in the world had been affected by the rotation of the human mind towards the future, the Foreign Office has remained immune. There, at any rate, war was what it always had been. You fought your way to your enemy's capital and you then "dictated terms." The objective of a war was victory. To reveal your terms beforehand was not done. So the Foreign Office never committed itself to a binding endorsement of our War Aims Memorandum, and it never warned us of various secret understandings that affected it. It remained in the self-satisfying pose of a superior body tolerating us and using us according to the best diplomatic traditions. And at length at Versailles the terms were dictated.

Until the German capitulation we went on with our development of the League of Nations movement, committing ourselves to very definite promises to the German

[1] See *Secrets of Crewe House* by Sir Campbell Stuart.

people, in the hope that our engagements would be honored at the Peace. They were not honored. We had taken the utmost pains in our propaganda to distinguish between the German people and the Hohenzollern government, and to hold out hopes of a speedy return to the fellowship of nations and a reasonable prospect of recuperation to a chastened and republican Germany. The victorious Foreign Offices treated all that as new-fangled rubbish. The Quai d'Orsay in particular seemed obsessed with a dream of obliterating Germany, of dividing it up so that it would never reassemble itself. They continued to kick Germany about until Germany became frantic with shame and hate, until Germany passed from reason to screaming fury. Its screaming fury found its incarnation at last in Hitler. He did not hesitate at the thought of war. He demanded war. He did not hesitate at the possibility of a subsequent social revolution. The victors of Versailles found Red Revolution even more terrifying than flaming war, and he played upon that terror. They passed from arrogance to propitiatory terror. This madman, they felt, might do anything. History became an attempt to humor and appease a lunatic who after all—and that was the worst of it for them—was not always quite so mad as he seemed.

All that is now quite familiar to everyone. What concerns us more directly here are those meetings and movements and discussions that occurred when the idea of the League of Nations was being shaped. These deliberations brought home to me the confused divergence of historical preoccupations among those taking part in them. Their minds were full of broken scraps of history, irrational political prejudices, impossible analogies. Everyone saw the idea from a different angle and seemed prepared to realize it by the hastiest of compromises. *The Outline of History* was the direct outcome of the experience I gathered in these discussions. At first, in conjunction with L. S. Woolf [1] and one or two others, I tried to organize a Research Committee, which would set itself to think out the full significance and possibilities of this great idea. We made William Archer, who was badly out of a job just then, the salaried secretary of this body. With much internal friction we compiled *The Idea of a League of Nations, Prolegomena to the Study of World Organization,* and *The Way to the League of Nations: A Brief Sketch of the Practical Steps Needed for the Formation of a League.* These booklets are still available for the collector. Then President Wilson came to Europe and we were swept aside, because he had his own ideas, and very crude ideas they were, of a League that would make the world safe for democracy. But the difficulty of producing these two reports opened my eyes to the enormous obstacles in the way of all volunteered co-operation. It seemed impossible to hold a team together. They differed upon endless points and they would not come together to hammer them out. They were all too intent upon what they considered more immediately important things. Our chief financial supporter deserted us to go off wool-gathering upon his own lines.[2] He could not see what need there was for all this highbrow research. But we were all going off upon our own lines. We had already disintegrated before we were disregarded.

At a conference with some representative Americans at

---
[1] Author of an excellent book, *International Government* (1916).
[2] See *Note* 9A expanding this.

the Reform Club during the war, I pointed out the urgent need for a general history of mankind which would consolidate people's ideas about the establishment of some sort of World Pax. Everyone thought it was a good idea. But here again was something which was nobody's business in particular. There was no time to go about collecting, persuading and editing the academically right people. One might as well have asked Lord Acton to write something. An Outline of History had to be done soon, even if it had to be flung together—and, getting help wherever I could find it, I flung one together.

I did it as well as I could, I worked enormously, and the strenuous hostile criticism to which it has since been subjected has revealed hardly any serious errors of statement. But a lot of it was headlong writing. It seemed to me at the time that if I and a few people could show that there was a shape to history, then it would be easy, since there is no copyright in the past, for the professional historians to rectify any serious flaws and do it better. They did nothing of the sort, and, failing that better performance, *The Outline of History* was launched upon a world conspicuously in need of just that assemblage of information. It had a fantastic success. Millions of copies have been sold and it has been translated into practically every important language in the world—except Italian. Fascist Italy could not tolerate the candid criticism of the Roman Empire.

I was probably rather excited by this astonishing boom. I do not know about that because I was not watching myself very closely. But I think that even at the time I did realize that this immense sale was no tribute to my authorship. It was something much more significant. It was the revelation of a world-wide hunger for adequately summarized knowledge on the part of multitudes whom the schools had sent empty away.

It seemed to me that this aching void probably extended far beyond the field of history. I knew that the general public throughout the world was being kept in the blackest ignorance of modern biological knowledge, evolutionary thought, modern ideas about individuality and modern psychology. I have already told in the Introduction how I realized that in my own case. With the assistance of Dr. Julian Huxley and my son, G. P. Wells, I produced a far more competent companion volume to *The Outline of History*, *The Science of Life*. It is fuller and more searching and better done than its predecessor, but its success was by no means astronomical.

Then I turned to the most difficult and original of all these encyclopædic essays, *The Work, Wealth and Happiness of Mankind*. This was an attempt to rescue social, economic and monetary "science" from the medieval scholasticism, the theorizing unworldliness, in which it still wanders. It was also an attempt to get behind the arbitrary assumptions upon which the Marxist doctrine of a necessary class war is based. Instead of jumping into the matter in the accepted academic style from some crudely plausible assumption, I approached these questions as a special branch of human ecology, and opened the matter out from a realistic survey of human life as a going concern. I began with a survey of the substances and power in the service of man, and thence I pursued a series of interrogations, How? and Why? up to government and education.

It was a laborious task; I chose some unsuitable collaborators from whom I had to disentangle the enterprise with considerable expense and difficulty; but in the end I managed to get every section of it "vetted" by authorities of the first rank. It is sound and tested matter.

In the end the book failed to earn the attention I think it deserved. The title may have been unpromising to the ordinary reader, the manner of its marketing unsuitable. It might have had better fortune as An Outline of Social and Economic Knowledge. I am convinced there is as great a public ready for a summary of facts and ideas upon social, political and monetary matters as there is for historical and biological digests. The book did not get to them. The world of economists and so forth ignored it completely—but then it is their practice also to ignore one another completely, to ignore almost everything completely. I find a sort of recognition of it in Barbara Wootton's brilliant *Lament for Economics* (1938), for which I am discouraged enough to be grateful. She is not biologically trained, she is probably quite ignorant of general ecology, but her realization that economics has still to become a science and can only become a science by admitting the descriptive treatment and examination of actual things and processes, is perfectly clear.

One other book I must mention here. *The Salvaging of Civilization* was written originally to be delivered as lectures in America, a project frustrated by a bout of influenza. Therein, borrowing a phrase from Dr. John Beattie Crozier,[1] I launched the idea of a "Bible" for civilization. In this idea of a "Bible" for the new social and political order, it is plain that Dr. Crozier and myself are groping our way and getting very near to a full realization of the scale and nature

[1] See *Note* 9B for his dates and two chief works.

of the mental readjustment incumbent upon the world. This new "Bible" of ours is the World Encyclopædia, to which I am coming, in embryo. I will not recapitulate the various other papers, pamphlets, books, with which I documented my successive mental readjustments, because they are ceasing to have anything more than a minor, personal significance. I was traveling along a road that a number of my contemporaries were following.

Step by step the more responsive elements in my generation were being forced towards a complete recognition of the need for a realistic preparation for the future, if our existence henceforth was to be anything better than a mechanical response to the blows of adverse fate that were beating upon us now, faster and faster. We were asking "What shall we do?" and more realistically "What have we to do?" and it was plain that the answers to these questions needed setting down as the necessary articles of association for a world-wide revolutionary effort. There may have been a slight slackening of this mental fermentation during the phase of the Fatuous Twenties, but it was revived with the mounting sense of urgency that came with the Frightened Thirties. Crisis appeared following crisis, each more menacing than the last—it was like the Pacific surf coming in before a rising gale—and what had we prepared for these crises?

By the early thirties I was one of those who were becoming fully aware that the systematic reconditioning of our mental life was not a secondary but a primary need for all mankind. It has beyond all question become now the most urgent and important thing in the world.

And also I was realizing the unsatisfactoriness of such detached, unco-ordinated work as writers of my type were doing. A number of us were all saying very much the same sort of thing, but without much co-ordination or anything mutual in the way of consequences. We could plead that we were pioneering and exploring, but that is merely a provisional plea. There comes a time to have done with sketches and samples. There is a quantitative element in real affairs. Doing something does not amount to very much unless you do enough.

The achievement of the French Encyclopædists has always appealed very strongly to my imagination. Diderot and his associates had scented the onset of change; they had set themselves, in the measure of their times, to prepare and equip the ideology of the new world they anticipated. They worked against great difficulties and within hampering limitations, but they did produce a new, inspiring conception of a world renewed. They gave a definite form and direction to the confused and powerful liberal impulses of their time. Their assembled thought materialized in the American and French revolutions and in a great heartening of the creative spirit of man throughout the whole world. They lived in an age of comparatively small things. The public capable of understanding and transmitting their ideas was a limited one. But it became very clear to me that what was needed in the face of the oncoming challenges of our time was essentially a new Encyclopædism commensurate with the relative vastness of our new occasions.

I set myself to the development of this idea of a modern Encyclopædism which should assemble facts and suggestions with the same insistence upon scientific reality and the same exclusion of irrelevances that has controlled the establishment of the world outlook I have put before the reader.

In a small book, *World Brain* (1938), the reader will find the substance of my proposals stated more fully and explicitly than is convenient here. I would be glad if the reader could find time to get and read it. I have made a sort of campaign for this new Encyclopædism and I continue to work for it to the best of my ability. *World Brain* is a book, quite bold and uncompromising in substance, but still with a distinctly propitiatory manner. It makes clear and definite proposals for a world-wide reconstruction of what we call higher education. What I call the permanent World Encyclopædia is projected as a permanent institution, a mighty super-university, holding together, utilizing and dominating all the teaching and research organizations at present in existence. This is shown to be not only a plausible and practicable idea, but an idea already finding a material embodiment in part and detail, through the common-sense needs of the scientific and technical world. A permanent World Encyclopædia, as I show in that book, is indeed crystallizing into existence, but at a pace altogether too slow for the urgency of the human situation. Bound up with this in the same book is a frank survey of what the citizen of a modern democratic world should know—that is to say, a scheme for an adequate modern education. This survey constituted my address as President of the Education Section of the British Association at Nottingham in 1937. It is much more provocative in its manner than the Royal Institution lecture of which it forms the complement. It

## SAMPLE OF A GENERATION 79

completely excluded both the Bible mythology and national and imperial history from the educational scheme.

Throughout 1937 I was doing what I could to promote this new Encyclopædism I had in mind, but with very little effect, and in the autumn I went to America and lectured, as *World Brain* relates. There is no need to recapitulate that American discourse here, but what is very apparent to me as I re-read the book, is the sacrifice of intensity in the effort to make it interesting and attractive. I am trying out ways and means in a very discursive spirit. I attempt some disarming jests. I write as though there was still quite sufficient time in hand to bring about the new mental orientation. I still had that feeling. Taking myself as a fair sample of the more progressive thought of my time, it is plain that up to the publication of *World Brain* in the spring of 1938 we were still not fully aware of the nearness of a culminating crisis in human affairs.

That forced itself upon our attention in spite of ourselves. We were compelled by the rush of circumstances to realize not only the unqualified soundness, but also, what is by no means the same thing, the urgent and fundamental importance of our intellectual convictions.

In the summer I was invited to be the guest of the Australian and New Zealand Association for the Advancement of Science at Canberra, and this involved giving an hour's discourse. I was becoming more and more impatient with the failure of the new encyclopædia idea to secure any energetic support, and also I was growing more and more impatient with my own personal ineffectiveness in the matter. I determined to use this invitation to assert still more plainly and clearly—to myself among other hearers—the case for a new encyclopædia and a radical revision of the world's educational organization. In Canberra I gave this address the title of *The Role of English in the Development of the World Mind,* for reasons I have set out in a note at the end of this book.[1] I repeated this lecture with some slight modifications as a public lecture in Sydney Town Hall, under the title of *The Human Outlook.* Substantially this book is an expansion of that address. Its line of thought is the same; its conclusions are the same. It is fuller, much more explicit and more closely reasoned, and its application to current affairs is closer and, to my mind, inescapable.

In addition I volunteered to read another paper to the Education Section at Canberra. I called it *A Provocative Paper on the Poison called History.* This also was made into a very largely attended public lecture, at which debate would have been impossible. It was an hour's show. As I wanted to bring whatever opposition there might be to my thesis into the light of clear statement, I suggested that the Education Section should provide time for its discussion.

The reception of these lectures and addresses was very typical of the transitional state of mind in which we are all living, even the most enlightened of us. They were, you must take my word for it, vividly successful. They were delivered in a setting of compliments and applause. I had been stimulating, amazingly stimulating. I had said things that had long needed saying. I had given them all food for thought of the most invigorating kind. Distinguished men of science came to thank me earnestly for the plainness of my statements. And so on.

[1] For the advantages of English see *Note* 9c.

And then everything went on just as it had been going on before. The stimulant seemed to evaporate at once and the food was certainly not assimilated.

The Right Honorable William Hughes, that distinguished Australian statesman, had very kindly consented to preside over my Town Hall lecture and at the end of it he expressed his appreciation. "God save us all," he said, and then, advancing to the front of the platform, he led the audience with the singing of "God Save the King." Everybody stiffened up to attention. I had been stating as lucidly as I could the reasons for believing that the human species was already staggering past the zenith of its ascendancy and on its way through a succession of disasters to extinction. And then we shook off the disagreeable vision, and lifted up our voices in simple loyalty to things as they are.

The discussion of that "provocative paper" by the Education Section was still more remarkable. I had denounced the teaching of the Judæo-Christian mythology as historical fact, in the most emphatic terms. Not a single Christian teacher appeared to reply to that challenge. Most of them, including the masters in one or two progressive schools who had been most anxious to turn my publicity value to account, contrived to have a parallel conference with another Section. In place of a discussion upon the crucial points I had sharpened, we had a series of brief, disconnected addresses by various educational officials, public characters and thoughtful people, about education in general, speaking in an elevated and discursive spirit, making many admirable but irrelevant philosophical remarks and including much autobiographical material. The avoidance of the essential issue was complete. And it was quite deliberate. The discussion was over and nothing had come of it and things were still very agreeably as they always had been. Tea was ready.

Now these were not consciously backward people. They knew indeed that they were the elite of Australasian progress. These Associations for the Advancement of Science throughout the world, the British, the American and the Australasian, are essentially assemblies of well-informed and liberal and progressive minds. But the real world of our Conference was still this wholly present world in which there are parents to consider, promotion to consider, dismissals, retirements, a world of knighthoods and honors. I went away pondering these things. Presently—let me confess it, lest I seem to claim to be anything better than a sample of a generation—I found myself discussing rather keenly the terms upon which I would lecture in Sydney.

Plainly we are not moving fast enough. We are still balancing in this strange phase of indecision between the actual present and the inevitable future. Even what we may call the more advanced intelligences vacillate and fail to sustain their constructive faith. The established, habitual present remains their real world. They may be profoundly disturbed—intellectually. They may be greatly unsettled and alarmed by the ever-increasing uncertainty of life, but still, in the exact sense of the word "realize," they fail to realize the urgent, implacable future. As the legendary gentleman who sat over his drink in the bar of the sinking *Titanic* remarked: "Well, anyhow, the damn thing hasn't gone down *yet*."

They are all continually relapsing towards acceptance of the prevalent contemporaneous outlook because that is what is most natural in the normal human make-up. At any sign of respite they yield to it. Alertness to the future, we have to realize, is a novel and artificial thing in life. It has to be constantly refreshed and sustained. Minds must be trained and accustomed to it; it is a matter of social atmosphere much more than individual intelligence. They have to be held up to it by something stronger and more permanent than themselves.

It is only in such an educational organization as I have been deducing from our present needs and, I hope, forecasting here, in such a permanent organization of knowledge, systematically assembled, continually extended and renewed and made freely and easily accessible to everyone, that there is the slightest hope of our species meeting the serried challenges of destiny that advance upon it. It is impossible to be steadily futuristic, solo, without a sustaining social organization which will give as assured and habitual a quality to the forward orientation of the everyday life as is now possessed by the unprogressive world of today.

And that organization fails to materialize.

I am impatient and at the same time I do not know how to accelerate matters. I do not think this is simply a case of the distress of an old man in a hurry. There is every justification for hurry in the world about us. I think that however young and hopeful I might be, I should still be intensely impatient to see this movement for human re-education quickened and implemented.

This reconditioning and reorientation of the human mind has to be undertaken not merely against the innate resistances to changing conditions in everyone's make-up. These innate resistances are organized very powerfully and effectively, and the nature of their organization is one we have now to examine. And also we are working against time. It is this time factor that casts the darkest shadow upon the possibility of a single, clear-headed, creative, happily interested, war-free human community emerging from the returning chaos of the present to dominate our planet through long ages still to come.

Years ago I threw out a sentence that caught the attention of that very great and lucid historian, James Harvey Robinson. He picked it up and repeated and commended it and gave it a wide publicity. The outlook for mankind, I had written—I think in *The Salvaging of Civilization*—is "a race between education and catastrophe."

Today catastrophe is well on its way, it is losing no time at all, but education seems still unable to get started, has indeed not even readjusted itself to start. The race may, after all, prove a walk-over for disaster.

## 10

### ESTIMATING HOPE

HERE A PERSONAL FACTOR comes in, which, I think, should be explained to the reader.

We are now in a field of thought from which it is impossible to banish a temperamental estimate of values. I find a certain defeatism has invaded my mind in the course of the past year. I anticipate very little happiness in the residue of my life. I feel that the odds are very heavily against any such educational revolution being even attempted in my lifetime—there will be no Pisgah glimpse of the promised world for me—and that in all probability my last years will be passed in a very ugly and distressful phase of human history. In many quarters I am unlikely to be a *persona grata*. A spell of ill-health involving bodily discomfort and a considerable ebb of mental resilience is contributing to this depression. These are my circumstances.

That matter of health is comparatively a minor issue. But quite apart from any bodily depression, the spectacle of evil in the world during the past half-dozen years—the wanton destruction of homes, the ruthless hounding of decent folk into exile, the bombings of open cities, the cold-blooded massacres and mutilations of children and defenseless gentle people, the rapes and filthy humiliations and, above all, the return of deliberate and organized torture, mental torment and fear to a world from which such things had seemed wellnigh banished—has come near to breaking my spirit altogether.

Said an old friend of mine the other day: "If only we could get away from events for a spell! If only we could get together as we used to get together and laugh!"

Children still laugh. Laughter is born again in each generation. What is past is over and done with for those who did not share in it. Life begins again incessantly. The sequence of birth and death is a continuing amnesty, but for my generation there have been things so unforgettable and disappointments so bitter that for us laughter has become almost a brutality. The dead past is dead—but not for us. We have been too near it and we are splashed with blood.[1]

It is well to remind the reader that though all that follows is written as objectively and truly as I can, it is overshadowed by these misadventures of my generation and mental type. The younger the reader is the more he or she should be able to discount the discouragement of our shadows.

And a consideration he must bear in mind in weighing what I am putting before him is the probability that there is a kind of egotistical intolerance in every definitely elderly mind. That is almost inevitable. Through a long life a complex system of ideas is built up upon a framework of concepts and associations determined by early circumstances. One qualifies, modifies, extends, superimposes significance upon this primary structure, but after a time it becomes irreplaceable. It may not be the best possible foundation, but

[1] See *Note* 10A for a schoolgirl's reaction to A.R.P.

## ESTIMATING HOPE

the more it has to carry, the less it can be changed. It is like a business that has grown up in reasonably convenient premises, they might be better laid out perhaps, but there is no possibility now of completely revising the lay-out. The going concern must carry on. But it becomes more and more difficult to rephrase one's ideas or to recognize them when they are rephrased. So that I may be much less alone and outstanding than I am disposed to think.

The nearer my beliefs are to reality the more probable it is that similar minds may be traveling along parallel, if not identical, lines of thought to practically the same conclusions, approached perhaps from a different starting-point and so differently phrased. I suspect and indeed I hope that I do not allow fully for that.

For example, there is the peculiar dialect of so many minds in the war generation who resorted to communism and the Communist Party to express their recoil from the existing state of affairs. It was the handiest formula for any sort of organized dissent. Many of them—not all, alas!—are emerging to a broader conception of what can be done with life, but they still speak with a strong Marxist accent. Some few, and my friend J. B. S. Haldane is among their number, seem to be resolved like Lenin (but without the justification of his circumstances) to read a wisdom and profundity into the sage of Highgate which was certainly not there. His Haldane Memorial Lecture (Birkbeck College, May 24th, 1938), was, to my mind, a brilliant yet obstinately perverse overvaluation of the role of Marx (and Engels) in human thought, which may well have made the worthy uncle whom he was commemorating turn in his grave. Lord Haldane also professed the Hegelian faith and that was his nephew's justification. This lecture made the most of Marx, I insist, and more also. And then more.

Now I have always had a peculiar contempt and dislike for the mind and character of Karl Marx, a contempt and dislike that have deepened with the years. I have given it the liveliest expression I could contrive in "The Shaving of Karl Marx" in *Russia in the Shadows* and in the "Psychoanalysis of Karl Marx" in *The World of William Clissold*. My only regret for these brief essays is that I could not infuse more sting and challenge into them. I have watched the tradition of Marxian bad manners and Marxian dogmatism wrapping like a blanket of fog round the minds of two crucial generations. They seemed to me to be lost in the fog. It was difficult for me to think they could be advancing under that fog.

Yet when, for example, I turn over such a book as *The Social Function of Science* by that very considerable writer, Professor J. D. Bernal, F.R.S., I get at times, in spite of his very distinct Marxist twang, a curious sense of parallelism and co-operation. And much that J. B. S. Haldane said in his lecture, I find as I read it over again, I could subscribe to, except that I reject the Marxist attribution.

I am reminded of the story of an Englishman who had a more or less rudimentary cultural conversation with a Japanese gentleman. The latter broke into an oration, a gabble, a flow of unfamiliar sounds which sounded like no known human speech. Then something clicked over in the hearer's mind. He made some rapid transpositions and light broke upon him. He was hearing one of the most familiar of Shakespeare's speeches in English! English of a different tint.

## ESTIMATING HOPE

I have been asserting, in a phraseology that no doubt owes much more than I realize to the phrases and assumptions of the liberal, protestant, progressive world of half a century ago, a view of the human outlook, that seems to me to be irresistibly convincing if one accepts a known series of facts. The truer and more inevitable that view is, the more probable it is that intelligent men, starting from all sorts of different standpoints, will converge upon the same conclusions. In English of a different tint. Indeed, it will be the completest disproof of my contentions, if there is not that convergence, if my conclusions do not reappear independently, crop up from a variety of starting-points and yet work out towards practically the same pattern. If the compelling facts do, as I assert, lie plainly on the face of things, that must be so. But probably, because I have a phraseology of my own, I shall be among those least able to recognize it.

And another thing that anyone who has spent most of his mental energy in trying to give the fullest and most emphatic expression to the truth as he perceives it, may easily underrate, is the tacit insubordination of many of the suppressed and formally silenced minds who are apparently disciplined against us. It is well to recall that all that outbreak of liberal questioning, the Protestant Reformation, which did so much to prepare the way for the French Revolution, was due almost entirely to the mental insurrection of friars or priests. They had had to take their creeds seriously, and they had brooded over their dogmas until they found them unbearable. There was no effective attack from without upon Church teaching throughout the whole Reformation period. There were close at hand in the alien disbeliefs of Jew and Moslem, a tacit denial of the Catholic faith, but these provoked no reforming zeal. All that came from within. And conversely the Jesuit Counter Reformation was the work of a group of romantic-minded laymen led by a court-bred gallant who had been wounded and crossed in love. The seven founders of the Society of Jesus were with one exception laymen. They were excited outsiders. They believed crudely and without qualification. They had had none of that intimate instruction of the mind from which questionings arise. They were, so to speak, the Nazis of Roman Catholicism.

But that is a passing comment. The more relevant point is the indisputable, obstinate tendency of common sense to assert itself in minds deliberately trained in any elaborate system of intolerance and error. Fanatics are madmen who find a masochist pleasure in strangling their own doubts, there is no dealing with them; but wherever there is discussion and mental training there lurks in every organized dogmatism a class of potential rebels. Hidden allies and half-hearted antagonists may be waiting to come over to a movement for the radical reconstruction of human ideology as it gathers strength. They are, so to speak, among the undisclosed reserves of progress.

Moreover, in further mitigation of my defeatist mood, it has to be borne in mind that while there is still life in a species no biological defeat is complete. Men and women of my type of mind and my generation, however the odds work against us, have no alternative to a stoical persistence in our convictions until our courses are run. We may have to admit regretfully a loss of buoyancy and of the ability for flexible mental co-operations. That is our private affair. In that we are just as much war casualties as those who may

## ESTIMATING HOPE

have suffered physical disablement in battle but are not yet completely incapacitated. Our injuries narrow down the scope of our service, but they furnish no justification for abandoning a loyal participation in the struggle. Our cause may still be winning.

Finally, as to the urgency of all this, let it be remembered that nothing is more difficult than estimating possibilities in time, and that timing here is a factor of primary importance. Disaster seems to me to be advancing upon us, but it may be that I am overlooking or underestimating the possibility of some intercalary slowing-down in the pace of change. I may be failing to perceive possible delaying forces. Some unexpected development of anti-aircraft technique might, for example, greatly minimize the destructiveness of air raids and the possibility of surprise wars.[1] The world may be held back from disaster for a time by the very weight and strain of its own armaments. It may be false to assume that sooner or later guns will go off of their own accord. Guns can rust and explosives disintegrate. A balance of power may be possible for longer years than I suppose, heavy and burthensome years perhaps, but still not years of complete catastrophic collapse.

In that pause, many people will be thinking hard, and the human intelligence may find methods of discussion and organization unknown to us. I find myself unable to imagine any such respite, and so I cannot bring it honestly into my account-rendered of the world, but there may be such a possibility. That gives no excuse for slackening, but it does justify a certain hopefulness.

With that I think I can finish with myself as a typical

---

[1] See *Note* 10B for such a possibility.

sample in evidence in this survey of the reaction of *Homo sapiens* to his present dangers. These ego-centered passages are not really so egotistical as they will seem to be to the antagonistic reader. It is auto-vivisection. I was by far the best and handiest rabbit for this demonstration.

Allowing for my own loss of individual hopefulness and that probable narrowing down of co-operative tolerance in my mind, the conclusions I am presenting to you remain nevertheless sound, grimly sound. The prospect for our species is just as stern and implacable, charged just as much with bracing uncertainty. The issue upon which I am in doubt is not whether I am right or wrong about the facts I have assembled; it is simply whether you of the new generation can be sufficiently braced in time. There, maybe, I do you an injustice. That is what I am saying.

What I have admitted in qualification of my own ebb of confidence, is no justification whatever for mere optimistic trumpetings—"I believe in the ultimate triumph of civilization"—and so forth. We have heard so much of that kind of hysteria. Without personal and organized devotion it means less than nothing. It is desertion under cover of a declaration of faith.

There are always plenty of well-meaning people in the world ready to relax at the slightest encouragement, and the surest preparation for disaster is the enervation of sentimental overconfidence. Face your adversary at his worst and most menacing, and then you will know best how to set about him. Rational adaptation, I admit, may be achieved ultimately, but only heroically, at a great cost. The odds are against it, rest assured, if not perhaps so heavily against it as nowadays they seem to be, to me.

## 11

### SURVEY OF EXISTING FORCES

WE ARE NOW IN a position to reconsider the nature of the various established systems that block the way to the readjustment of the human species as one single, continually progressive and creative world community, and to make a rough estimate of the way in which they are operating at the present time. We arrive with minds cleansed and refreshed by our survey of the biological situation, at the political, social and religious realities of today.

Legally the world's affairs are in the control of a miscellany of sovereign states, and each embodies itself in a government of politicians and officials, deeply concerned in maintaining the bargaining autonomy of the particular regime which gives them their importance, and prepared to offer a spirited resistance to any invasion, conquest or amalgamation of brave little (or big or old) Ruritania, or whatever state it is. That is how the political map of the world presents things to us. But very few of these legal governments are real cultural entities. It is only one or two sovereignties that embody a complete cultural system of their own. For all practical purposes the British Empire is such a system, with a curiously loose yet persistent will and tradition, sustained by a very distinctive literature of biographies, memoirs, collected letters and speeches and the like, and a quite definite religion—or religious substitutes—the Anglican compromise between Protestant and Catholic Christianity. Still more complete is the Nazi Germany of today, which indeed is now strenuously self-sufficient even to the extent of a distinctive science, art, literature, history, clothing, dietary of its own. But most of the other states play their game of international competition over a sort of map which does not necessarily correspond to their spheres of sovereignty. They are like estates, farms and fields spreading over a substratum of soils and geological formations.

It is to these underlying foundation realities of the world situation that we must first direct our attention.

As the facts assembled in *The Outline of History* showed very clearly, the expansion in size of the early empires (saving only Egypt with its Nile) was dependent upon two advances in communication, writing and road-making. These expanding empires of the second and first millennia B.C. put a great strain upon the tribal and petty national religions (which in those days included the science and morality) of the smaller states they incorporated. A working compromise was found in a sort of fusion of the absorbing and absorbed cultures. A rejuvenated religion was produced by a mutual modification of ceremony and myth. The corresponding gods of these syncretic religions adopted each other's names as aliases, or they became different "aspects" of a consolidated deity (theocrasia). A general similarity in these more primordial tribal cults greatly facilitated this syncretic process.

About these primordial religions we now have a considerable body of assured knowledge. And this is not—we must underline here—knowledge in dispute. It is not a collection of theories we are bringing into court; it is an assemblage of facts. What we have to cite here is no more questionable than the facts of evolution and ecology that have been assembled in the earlier sections of this book. It is indeed knowledge that is not made accessible to everyone; that is the default of our educational systems; it is steadfastly ignored by many people who find it inconvenient and distasteful; but that does not affect its truth.

We know that these early religions were systems of fear and propitiation, that they centered upon the primary importance of a seasonal blood sacrifice, and that that sacrifice was the function of a priesthood, which was also in charge of the calendar and of whatever medical knowledge existed. From *The Golden Bough* of Sir James George Frazer, O.M., and from *Forerunners and Rivals of Christianity,* by F. Legge (published by the Cambridge University Press), the unbiased reader can realize for himself how this cannibal blood sacrifice has been refined at last into the Mystery of the Mass, which will indeed have very little mystery left for him if he faces the facts these writers, with no unnecessary emphasis nor any partisan purpose, put plainly before him.[1]

These investigations into the beginnings of religion have accumulated steadily throughout the past half-century. It is only by great efforts of censorship, by sectarian education of an elaborately protected sort and the like, that ignorance about them is maintained.

These seasonal blood-sacrifice religions had a wide range of local variation, their theogonies differed widely—in some

[1] See *Note* 11A.

of them, mystical, secret mother-nature goddesses lurked behind the great father god; in others, the totem animal prevailed—but in all their forms they sustained the fear-begotten idea of blood salvation. Two dozen centuries ago they were already suffering through the pressure not only of syncretic necessity but from the increasing skepticism of the awakening human intelligence. They still cumbered the earth with a multitude of temples and priesthoods, for where there is an endowment you can always find someone to be a priest, but they were producing complex developments of their theological explanations.

Ptolemaic Alexandria was a hot-bed of religious elaboration. At the Serapeum, before the middle of the third century B.C., it had produced a trinity with a sacrificial son, who is slain and ascends to the Father and becomes the Father. There were a regular and secular clergy, monks with tonsures, a choral Easter ceremony; and the worship of the goddess Isis bearing the infant Horus in her arms anticipated the Catholic adoration of the Virgin Mary down even to minor details. The hymn "Sun of my Soul, thou Saviour dear," addressed originally to the hawk-sun-god Horus, has become a Christian hymn. In the temples one saw collections of ex-votos hung up in gratitude for miraculous cures and escapes, and the ceremonial purchase and burning of votive candles was encouraged. The hope of a glorious immortality—which was little stressed in the earlier religions outside Egypt—was a central fact in this religious scheme, and so, too, was an insistence upon the material resurrection of the (in Egypt usually pickled) body. All this was going on nearly three centuries before there was a Christian in the world.

## SURVEY OF EXISTING FORCES

But very few Christians know these facts. They are all to be found fully documented in Legge (op. cit.).

We must turn now to a second factor in the basis of the cultural life of Europe and the Europeanized world, the Sacred Book.

While religious cults were limited in their range and appealed at most to a few thousand votaries, it was possible to sustain them by direct teaching and initiation, but as greater empires grew with the development of writing and land and sea communications, there appeared a new demand and also a new facility for mental organization. This was the written word. Spreading over the old sacrificial paganism, there presently appeared what one may distinguish as Book religions. Every great religion in the world today, whether it does or does not preserve the tradition of the cannibalistic blood sacrifice, is a Book religion.

The first of the Sacred Books to affect the Western world was the collection of Hebrew writings constituting the core of what is now called the Old Testament. It came into existence as a natural result of the series of misfortunes that happened to the various communities speaking the closely related Semitic languages which had dominated the Western world a thousand years before the Christian era. These were the Babylonian, Phœnician and Carthaginian states, the Jews who had been deported to Babylon and then returned to Palestine, and a variety of trading colonies and settlements in association with these Semitic-speaking centers. In the course of a few centuries these highly civilized and intelligent trading empires and cities, in common with various other old-world communities, collapsed under a series of barbarian raids and conquests coming from the

North. Most of these Northern barbarians spoke languages of the Aryan group. Between the Homeric Age and the third century B.C. they had, as the Persians, the Greeks and Macedonians, the Romans and Gauls, become masters of the larger part of the Mediterranean world, leaving the less warlike, Semitic-speaking peoples, *inter alia,* subdued and scattered and defeated but still trading, sustaining a financial network, navigating the seas and going to and fro in the world. They remained in possession of these roles because they knew more about them. The conquerors, as they became civilized, availed themselves, with a certain suspicion and resentment, of these superior gifts and facilities of the defeated. The Semitic business methods were ready-made for the new kings and aristocrats and warriors. They learnt to use them slowly and left them largely in Semitic hands.

During the course of these conquests there was naturally a great intermingling of blood. The subjugated Semitic and pre-Semitic peoples were certainly in the majority in the Latin, Greek, Persian and Macedonian empires; history records no general ban upon intermarriage, and we can hardly doubt that the actual blood of the ruling Aryan-speaker was the smaller factor in that continually stirred-up mixture which is now the European and Europeanized world of today.[1]

But traditions were less easily assimilated. Throughout that millennium which culminated in the Roman Empire, in all the ports and cities there must have been groups of households and business organizations struggling to maintain a level of refinement and behavior higher than that of their rulers, and eager also to preserve their business cor-

---

[1] See *Note* 11B on the racial unity of mankind.

## SURVEY OF EXISTING FORCES

respondence and a sympathetic understanding with their kindred throughout this new world that had annihilated and discredited their separate religious systems. They needed a Book to unify them, they were ripe for a Book, and the Book was ready for them.

It was in Babylon and Judæa and in the towns of these regions that those Jewish sacred writings first appeared. They contained two overlapping versions of the old Babylonian cosmogony, together with the myths of the Creation, the Serpent-Enemy, the Fall, the Flood and the Tower of Babel. They also contained the story of a Promise and of a Chosen People who were destined to recover all and more than their ancient ascendancy. But at a price. These Chosen People had to keep themselves aloof from the Gentile world. They must preserve their precious distinctive habits and usages intact. They must remain aloof and enduring, until a promised Messiah came to lead Israel to its final triumph over the rest of mankind.

The appeal of these Scriptures to the needs and imaginations of these scattered peoples on the defensive must have been irresistible. In a century or so Carthaginians, Phœnicians, Babylonians disappear from history, and all over the world of their former activities the Jewish communities appear, centering upon the schools of Babylon and Jerusalem with a consolidating literature and a religion. In this stage they proselytized freely. Probably the proselytizing was chiefly among kindred and sympathetic Semitic-speakers, but there were also Tartar and other tribes which were won over. The blood-sacrifice tradition was sustained by the priests in the Temple until the fall of Jerusalem to Vespasian in 70 A.D. Then the sacrifices ceased and the Sacred

Book with its semi-authoritative accretions became the link of Jewry throughout the world. . . .

So the first of the great Book religions on which our civilization rests arose. Hard upon its diffusion followed Christianity, its unidentical twin.

Christianity began as a Jewish sect, as the Books of the New Testament tell very simply and clearly; it was still entirely Jewish after the Crucifixion; and it was only through the initiative of Saint Paul that the ranks of the elect were opened to the uncircumcised. After the Four Gospels, the New Testament is largely occupied with Paul's reconstruction of the Nazarene cult. It is all very plain to anyone who reads these books without theological prepossessions. His brilliant intelligence seized upon the idea of presenting Jesus as the sacrificial king of the blood-sacrifice tradition. Jesus, he declared, was the Lamb by whose blood we were saved—though as a matter of fact crucifixion is hardly a more bloody death than hanging. He had died, said Saint Paul, not only for the Jews but for all men who would accept his sacrifice. This, for the stricter Jews, was an intolerable relaxation of their divine bargain. But some, less profoundly convinced of the Messianic hope, realized the attractive quality of the Pauline teaching.

The medium of diffusion for Christianity remained for a time the scattered Jewish communities. Throughout the first and second centuries Judaism and its offshoot, Christianity, the latter becoming more and more Gentile and anti-Jewish, spread and bickered side by side throughout the whole extent of the Roman Empire. The pagan world, although it was also in a state of great social and religious unrest—the two things seem to be inseparable—had no comparable nexus for the production of alternative sacred writings that could stand up against the dissemination of these Judæo-Christian legends and mythology. So that these latter provided the written factor in the foundations of civilization throughout the entire Western world.

Later, another Book religion, Islam, swept for a time across the Mediterranean scene, with very considerable reactions upon medieval science and thought. But that influence, and the effects of a vast multitude, myriads indeed, of less distinguished "Sacred Book" cults, are outside our present discussion.

It is necessary to recall these well-known—though persistently neglected—facts here because they establish a general statement that what we may call roughly Western culture—the mental adaptation of mankind to social and political life, from the Pacific coast westward across the Atlantic to farthest eastern Russia, up to as late as the second Russian Revolution in 1917—was based upon an interrelated system of Bible-centered Book religions which had either obliterated or assimilated the more ancient blood-sacrifice cults.

Let us now review the chief forms these foundation religions take in our world today.

## 12

### THE JEWISH INFLUENCE

FIRSTLY, BECAUSE OF ITS illuminating quality, we must consider the progressive segregation of the Jewish community. It has diverted, wasted and sterilized an amount of ability and moral energy that mankind at large can ill spare. In the previous section we have shown how naturally it arose out of the state of world affairs of the centuries before and after the Christian era, and how the realistic genius of Saint Paul sought an escape from its perilous limitations. From the very beginning, there must have been men of vision among the Jews who realized and rebelled against the moral isolation to which they were being condemned, there must have been a continual seeping-away of individuals to the larger opportunities of the outer world, but the uncompromising tradition carried by the old Bible and the associated writings which grew into the Talmud has been sufficient to hold together a core of inassimilable and aggressive orthodoxy to this day clinging obstinately to every detail of ritual, behavior and avoidance that emphasized the central legend of a Chosen People.

It is this orthodox remnant and its behavior and influence, the repercussions it evokes and the dangers to which it has

## THE JEWISH INFLUENCE 103

exposed the whole Jewish community, which constitute the Jewish problem. There would be no distinctive Jewish question at all were it not for this remnant and its activities.

The whole question turns upon the Chosen People idea, which this remnant cherishes and sustains, which it is the "mission" of this remnant to cherish and sustain. It is essentially a bad tradition, and the fact that for two thousand years the Jews on the whole have been very roughly treated by the rest of mankind does not make it any the less bad. Almost every community with which the orthodox Jews have come into contact has sooner or later developed and acted upon that conspiracy idea. A careful reading of the Bible does nothing to correct it.

Every sort of man is disposed to get together with his own sort of people and prefer them to strangers. That is the natural disposition of our species, fair play to the outsider is one of the last and least assured triumphs of civilization, but the indictment against the Jewish community is that their religion of a Chosen People takes this universal human vice, justifies it and stimulates it to the form of a persistent organized attitude of self-exclusion from the common fellowship of the world.

Everywhere the same reaction occurs and everywhere the Jew expresses his astonishment. Not only Christians but Turks have resorted to pogroms. In contact with the Arab, the Koran-taught Arab from the desert, who shares the Jew's cosmogony, who practices similar dietetic taboos, who is equally free from Trinitarian theology and sacrificial bloodshed, and has indeed a much stronger claim to be called Semitic, the angry reaction to the theory and practice of a Chosen People, to the practice much more than the theory, is just as violent as it is in any other part of the world.

It is this Chosen People tradition and still more the habit of mind which betrays itself in those who have come under its influence, which is the ever-recurrent cause of the trouble. It seems to me beside the mark to look for any other.[1]

Estimates of the number of Jews in the world vary between fourteen and sixteen million. The latter figure is given by Louis Golding in *The Jewish Problem* and by Lewis Browne in the careful and scholarly work he has entitled so flippantly, *How Odd of God*. ("How odd of God to choose the Jews!"—W. N. Ewer.) This is not a very great total. They have and always have had abundant and well-cared-for families. Probably outside the range of definitely associated Jews, there has always been a much larger world of sympathetic kin, sharing and affected by the feelings of the stricter core, capable of co-operating with it and responding to modifications of the central idea, but gradually slipping away beyond recall.

As we have noted in § 11 (and see also *Note* 11B) most of us probably have a more or less considerable proportion of "Jewish" blood in our veins, using "Jewish" in the larger sense. But orthodox Judaism has always been a narrower and intenser strain. It has passed through phases of leakage and recovery. The Protestant Reformation was a phase of leakage. Browne doubts whether there were half a million Jews in Europe in 1600, "fewer than were to be found in Castile alone four hundred years earlier."

Of the sixteen million Jews today, Browne estimates that there cannot be more than four million who are strict ad-

---

[1] See *Note* 12A for a further discussion of this point.

herents to and observers of the Law and that perhaps another six million are what he calls semi-observant; they are lax about food and drink and the Sabbath, but when it comes to celebrating marriages, funerals, taking an oath and so forth they follow the ancient formulæ, they attend the main annual feasts, they pay their pew rents and do their full duty by the Jewish charities. They are very much like the Anglicans who don't go to Church very much but would never dream of being married in a registry office. Then comes another three million who have become entirely indifferent to the Law. They do not attack it, but they put it aside. Yet they cling as nationalists to the solidarity it has preserved through the ages. They are Reform Jews or Radical Nationalists, like the law-disregarding young Jews of Palestine. Mr. Browne is himself a Reform Rabbi and he can write incidentally:

"There are certain writers who become tremulously nostalgic and tender when describing the life of those pietist Jews. Ensconced in laurel-embowered English cottages, or seated in cafés on Montparnasse, such writers will wax ecstatic as they discourse on the effulgent 'mysticism' enhaloing the ghetto hovels. But that, I fear, is because they have never entered those hovels. Had they done so they would in all likelihood realize—unless sentimentality had too thickly blurred their sight—that life in them is not bathed in the lambent light of unearthly wisdom: that instead it is dark and scabrous with superstition."

The remaining three of these sixteen million Jews are rapidly ceasing to be Jews at all, and he notes with a sort of calm amazement that "a cult which has lasted for centuries could be shattered in a decade." The younger generation has been given equality in the U.S.S.R., excellent schools and a new and exciting creed. Nominally they remain Jews, and their language, Yiddish, is one of the national languages recognized by the Union. But Hebrew has vanished—the Law, the Promise and Jehovah!

And at this point Browne and I part company. Judaism may vanish in Russia under communism, he has to admit, but it will live on elsewhere not by virtue of its own quality but because of Gentile intolerance. He argues that Gentile intolerance makes the Jews and keeps them together. I argue that the Jews make themselves and that Gentile intolerance is a response to the cult of the Chosen People. To get down to ultimate things, we are in substantial agreement, I find, in that we desire a world, enlightened, scientifically administered, free, a world-wide new civilization open to everyone, where there will be neither Jew nor Gentile, bond nor free. Nevertheless we differ diametrically in our interpretation of the root cause of the Jewish problem, and as a consequence upon the question where the tentative for denationalization should begin. Thirteen million Jews—at least—still make the implacable Gentile the justification for their own persistence. They still hold to that hard core of national separatism in spite of the steady evaporation of every traditional religious justification. Yet they have a world-wide organization for calling off that attitude and the Gentiles have no corresponding representative network to speak for them to the same extent. The Holy See has recently condemned racialism very clearly and definitely. So has the White House. . . .

But let me go on with what I believe is the truer version of the Jewish story, and the reader, with a glance at the

## THE JEWISH INFLUENCE

notes at the end whenever he needs confirmation, must judge between me and the defenders of persistent Jewish nationalism.[1]

The hostile reaction to the cult of the Chosen People is spreading about the entire world today. In the past the Jews have been subjected to much resentful treatment and much atrocious cruelty and injustice, now here, now there, but there has never been such a world-wide—I will not use the word anti-Semitism because of the Arab—I will say anti-Judaism. Now, because of the physical unification of the world, the resentment against the theory and practice of a Chosen People is much quicker and more contagious than it used to be; it is becoming world-wide and simultaneous. The idea is becoming everywhere more and more intolerable than it has ever been before.

The cultivated, exaggerated, national egotism of the Chosen People has never been so conspicuous as it has been in the present century and particularly since the War. As their ritualism has weakened their nationalism has increased. I recall a conference that took place in '19 or '20 in a room in the House of Commons. A number of French writers had deputed Madame Madeleine Marx to discuss with various English men and women of letters the possibilities of concerted action and possibly organization in the cause of world peace and world understanding. In those days Israel Zangwill had adopted the role of Champion of the downtrodden and suffering Jewish race, and more particularly of that section of it which was to be found in the wealthier mansions of West Kensington and Tyburnia, *en route* from the East End to the House of Lords. He sustained its racial

---

[1] See *Note* 12B for that fuller discussion.

pride, if indeed that needed sustaining. He insisted upon Israel's distinction and its inappeasable hunger for restoration to the land of the protracted Promise. He told them of the *Dreamers of the Ghetto*. He reminded them of their origins with humor and emotion. He helped them to feel "different," as the American car salesmen say, and mystically better. They were, he persuaded them, not really having the good time they seemed to be having; behind the brave face they put upon things they were weeping by the waters of Babylon. The true voice of Israel was to be heard not in the West End of London but when it went off for a trip to Palestine and, following the customary routine, wailed at the Wailing Wall. Always he spoke of *"My* people."

He brought his championship to our deliberations. We various British authors had had our trivial shares in the "war to end war," and we were very willing to fall in with any proposals that would help to rationalize the heated and punitive atmosphere of the Versailles peace. We felt that a peace that would indeed end war was slipping away from us. But we found this conference dominated by the communist dogmatism of Madame Marx, against which Bernard Shaw protested, and Zangwill's preoccupation with his "people." He laid down the conditions that would satisfy their needs; he insisted on what would satisfy them, what would make them willing to help us, and the difficulties an offended Jewry could create for us. So far as I could grasp his drift he was dealing with us as the British Empire. We were not the British Empire, but it was vain to protest. Zangwill was a very resolute character and that was the drama he had in mind. Just as in our private disputes he would insist on treating me as a devout Christian. Then he could say: "But your Saviour was a Jew!" Useless to plead that I was not a Christian, and that there might be considerable prepotency in the Holy Ghost. Zangwill was being the captive nation making his terms with the oppressor. It is the drama so many people still have in mind when discussing this question.

In those days we in the victorious allied countries were all ready to believe that the world was really recovering from the War and entering upon a phase of comparative freedom and hope. We did our best not to think too much about the state of affairs in Germany. Everybody was talking of reconstruction and rationalization, and it was possible to deal jestingly with things that have now become intolerably grim.

The Zionist movement was the crowning expression of what I, in flat contradiction to Mr. Browne, hold to be the obdurate insistence of orthodox and semi-orthodox Jewry upon their peculiarity. In the years immediately following the war, there was a lull even in the normal persecutions in Eastern Europe to which the orthodox were subjected. They suffered indeed during the civil disorders that preceded the consolidation of the Bolshevik government; Whites, Reds and Greens were alike guilty of pogroms of varying degrees of virulence, and there was in consequence a certain exodus westward, but as the new law and order were established in Russia these outrages ceased and the process of rapid assimilation, to which reference has already been made, began. But already the champions of Judaism were advertising to the whole world how implacably they insisted upon their eternal essential foreignness. They had demanded a national home, so that elsewhere they could be forever foreigners. They might within limits accept the advantages of citizenship of the country they lived in, but essentially they would not belong. They would vote, hold office, rule, but always with Zion in their hearts. They ignored the manifest fact that the day of small sovereign states is drawing to an end, and that in a world of ever-growing violence, to plant themselves massively in any particular area was to invite a wholesale disaster.

Today when the whole world is being subtly pervaded with anti-Jewish feeling, and when the restraints upon the predatory and persecuting impulses in the human animal are being rapidly weakened, these implacable nationalists are still conspicuously seeking suitable regions where they can go on being a people by themselves, where, pursuing an ancient and irrational ritual so far as it suits them, they can sustain a solidarity foreign and uncongenial to all the people about them.

No country wants them on such conditions. Why should any country want these inassimilable aliens bent on preserving their distinctness? Palestine is an object lesson. Until they are prepared to assimilate and abandon the Chosen People idea altogether, their troubles are bound to intensify. No one can help them while even a die-hard minority—a minority that the general body of them does not disavow, a nucleus about which habit and association and sentiment gather very readily and to which it is easy for lost sheep to return—prefers these exasperating pretensions of a special right and claim to becoming frankly and of their own accord common citizens of the world.

These are the elementary facts of the quandary to which the Chosen People have come, the more relentless dragging the doubters and half-hearted with them. They are facts that have to be stated, even though matters are now coming

## THE JEWISH INFLUENCE

to a complexion which gives a flavor of ruthlessness to their bare statement.

Because this obdurate separatism which, after all, except for the growing trouble in Palestine, has been hitherto more of an irritant than a downright evil, is now conspicuous and challenging just at a phase in human affairs when it is becoming extremely dangerous to be in any manner alien and provocative.

In the last two paragraphs of § 4, the essential facts of the present rapid dislocation of social order have been stated. Social disintegration is now a world-wide reality, it is a convulsive breaking-down everywhere of long-established systems of law and order, an almost cataclysmal dissolution. It is a process far vaster than this Jewish question we are discussing and it arises from causes that have no special connection with that trouble. But it catches up the Jewish question in its swirling eddies and spins it about so that its fluctuations become indicative of the character of the entire process.

The Jewish question is already something very different from what it was a score of years ago when Zangwill championed and threw that glamor of racial romance and Maccabean heroism about the ancient ways. Those were tolerant days. At that time it was easy for people to fall away from the old observances if they chose and become Christians or unconforming skeptics. Now, and it is the most ominous aspect of the new phase, in many parts of the world the doors of escape from orthodox Jewry are being closed. These doors are not being closed from the inside; there is no way of closing them from the inside. They are being closed from the outside. Those who are disposed to apostasy are being turned back by the outer world. Nothing of this sort was happening twenty years ago. A number of people, and some of them are very sinister people indeed, are beginning to say, "You insisted upon being Jews. Jews you *shall* be."

The operating causes in those wide alternations between social confidence, a sense of stability and a prevailing lawfulness and intolerance, and phases of insecurity, fear, dishonesty and general unrighteousness, which have manifestly occurred in the human story, have still to receive anything but the most casual attention from the historian. Those happier periods, when the social machine was running smoothly, when men were able to move about freely and almost fearlessly, work with a sense of fair reward, when there was something definite and reasonably satisfactory and hopeful for most of the young men to do, have been by far the less frequent and the least secure. Order and peace have been precarious always in the growing human societies of the last four or five thousand years. There have been constantly recurrent phases of mutual pressure, expansion and that dislocation without which readjustment is impossible. Then doubt and suspicion invade men's minds. They lose that feeling that they are being properly taken care of; there is no confidence that services will be rewarded or debts paid; mutual trust gives way to suspicion. Social behavior deteriorates. The strong and cunning no longer feel that the weak will be protected. The suspicious look for scapegoats to blame, for evil doers who have offended the gods, for conspirators. Particularly for conspirators.[1]

We do know and we have already stated in general terms the forces that have produced the particular phase of

[1] See *Note* 12c for *The Protocols of the Elders of Zion*, etc.

## THE JEWISH INFLUENCE 113

violent social disintegration that is going on today. They are world-wide and unprecedented. Socially they are more destructive than anything our species has ever faced before. The disintegrating changes in the social order of the past were probably due to much more localized and quite different influences: to unrecorded fluctuations in the relative welfare of classes, to the social shifting due to new economic processes, to the infiltration of foreign ideas and practices, to foreign pressure, to epidemics—no history can be complete without a proper study of the social sequelæ of plague, the Black Death and the like—to sustained bad weather, drought for example, over a number of years, to a stimulating and disorganizing influx of gold such as happened after the discovery of America. These and a thousand other disturbing forces have been enough to tilt the always unstable and insecure social balance back to general distrust and convulsive, self-protective dishonesty. The adaptive culture fails. Things go to pieces. Man reverts to his more natural state of a fear-and-desire-driven beast.

In the history of any social system such periods of disorganization display almost parallel phenomena of demoralized mass action. The strong are looking for the weak not only individually but collectively in order to gratify their craving for power, the crowd is seeking the furtive enemies of the state, the fearful are looking for the strange wickedness and secret mischiefs that have brought about the discomforts of the time. In such an atmosphere any marked kind of people are liable to set upon, are liable to be ringed about for victimization and punitive plunder.

Such a convergence of hostility has by no means been confined to the Jews. The Albigenses, for example, in the south of France, had no very special relationship to the Jewish community. They were a Christian sect with certain heretical ideas derived by way of Bulgaria from the Gnostics and Manichæans. They were charged, by their exterminators, to whom we owe most of the knowledge we have of their beliefs, with abnormal sexual practices. What is more certain is that they protested vigorously against the corruptions of the Church and were markedly anti-sacerdotal. They spread throughout Provence and prospered throughout the twelfth century. Their movement was in several respects an anticipation of the Protestant Reformation. Whereupon the Church invoked the harder, ruthless and more Catholic north, and preached a Crusade against them. Moral and religious indignation and the prospect of loot implemented their destruction. Here we cannot tell the tale of massacres, burnings alive—two hundred in one *auto-da-fé*—the sadistic terrorism and blackmail of the Holy Inquisition. . . .

The Armenians again are another much massacred, non-Jewish but distinctive people.

But it is the Jews who have generally been the marked people throughout the realms of Christendom and Islam. They have generally "got it first." And repeatedly the door has been slammed upon Jews who have been seeking to get away or were actually getting away from the threats that darkened over them.

Lewis Browne gives a compact and effective account of the fate of the Marranos in Spain and Portugal. He tells of the forcible baptism and conversion of the Jews in 1391 in the face of a storm of popular hostility. The government, because of their financial and administrative usefulness, opened a door of escape for them. They were given the

## THE JEWISH INFLUENCE 115

choice between exile and massacre or Christianization. A great majority chose the latter, and since all the synagogues were closed and the practice of the Jewish law sedulously suppressed, within three or four generations most of these baptized Jews became just as good or better Catholics than their neighbors. This from the outset was a huge disappointment for those neighbors who had been whetting the knife, so to speak, for an orgy of murder and plunder. It seemed to them the meanest trick conceivable. They called these desperate converts the New Christians or more familiarly swine (=Marranos), and set as rigid a bar as possible on any intercourse with them. As Jews they had been "dogs" but now they were "swine." "Conversion indeed!" they said. "You don't get away with *that*."

In complete good faith the majority of the Marranos in the next generation or so were Catholics. "These hapless creatures," says Browne, "took no pride in their past. On the contrary they were through and through ashamed of it and groaned that it be forgotten." That did not help them in the least. Massacre and detailed persecution closed in on them. The tale is fully told in Mr. Cecil Roth's *History of the Marranos*. It is a frightful story, but from the point of view of the present discussion it is almost the same story, Inquisition and all, as that of the Albigenses who were not Jews at all.

An entirely parallel treatment has been meted out in the last decade to the Christian Jews in Germany. They have been herded back upon their orthodox brethren, in the same spirit and for the same reason that the Marranos were kept apart for destruction. We are witnessing now a swifter and vaster repetition of that Marrano tragedy.

A time has come when a multitude of men and women of more than average intelligence, men and women who in reality have no essential racial difference from the average European, are finding themselves with no foothold whatever upon the earth, dispossessed and hunted from country to country, marooned in impossible regions, deprived of the normal protection of the law, beaten up by anyone who chooses to beat them up, outraged, tortured, sterilized, stripped of everything, ill-treated in every possible way. They seek escape from one country to another, and the countries where they would take refuge, suffering now from the fast-spreading economic and social malaise of this current phase in human history, are more and more chary of receiving them even as assimilable individuals. Everywhere employment is dislocated. Everywhere they encounter the protest: "We have our own unemployed!"[1]

A great book, a book of victims with thousands of authenticated cases, could be filled already with the tale of forced suicides, murders and abominations done upon these refugees, and there is no reasonable prospect of surcease. From the narrower point of view the compilation might be called *The Jewish Book of Martyrs,* but from another it could be entitled *The Natural Man,* because its broader interest lies in the clear demonstration of what the inherent brute in man can do when the grip of law and order relaxes. It is a horrible recrudescence of primordial human reactions, but that is no reason why we should shut our eyes to the role of the alien nationalism of the Chosen People in exposing them first and foremost before any other people to this accumulating outbreak of hatred, cruelty, bestiality and

[1] See *Note* 12D upon the refugee question.

## THE JEWISH INFLUENCE

every sort of human ugliness. They are the first to suffer in the social dissolution of our epoch, because they have stood out most conspicuously. They are the most obvious "murderees" and "plunderees." They come first. But they are only the first. . . .

I have enlarged upon their case because it is not only conspicuously challenging at the present time but because it brings into the picture most of the elements of the present human situation, the general disposition of any established community to adhere to forms and traditions of living long after their survival value has disappeared, the normal blindness of human beings to the onset of novel and more exacting conditions until disaster actually supervenes, the swiftness with which social balance can now be overturned.

I can see no other destiny for orthodox Judaism and those who are involved in its obloquy, unless that enormous effort to reconstruct human mentality for which I have been pleading arrives in time to arrest their march to destruction. That, if it is to save our species, must be a reconstruction so bold and wide, an amnesty so fundamental, that it will sweep the religion of the Chosen People and this age-long feud of Juif and anti-Juif out of the living interests of mankind altogether.[1]

---

[1] For a practically identical view vividly expressed, read Wyndham Lewis's *The Jews, are they human?*

## 13

### CHRISTENDOM

FROM THE TRAGEDY OF Judaism we must turn now to Christianity, that second and greater branch of the Bible tradition, which is the basis of contemporary Western civilization. The word Christianity has covered and still covers an immense variety of idea systems, but today it finds its most highly organized and active expression in the Roman Catholic Church. That too is a power transcending national and state boundaries and playing a distinctive part in molding human thought and destiny today.

In certain respects Catholic Christianity is in diametric contrast to Judaism; in certain others the two cults run side by side. They have this in common that nearly everywhere they produce the feeling that they are alien cultures. They are apt to be suppressed by governments together, as in Hanoverian England and Hitlerian Germany, and to be emancipated together. But they differ fundamentally in the fact that while participation in Judaism after the early phase of eager proselytism became for many reasons difficult, Christianity from its beginning with Saint Paul (Acts xi, 26) onward has been a missionary religion, seeking and incorporating converts throughout the whole world.

It not only incorporated converts but it incorporated

# CHRISTENDOM

ideas. It sprang from the Jewish sect of the Nazarenes; but in the course of the three centuries before its forcible stabilization by Constantine the Great in 325 at the Council of Nicæa and the definitive formulation of its three creeds, the third-century Apostles' Creed, the fourth-century Nicene Creed, so much more explicit about the Trinity, and the Athanasian (of uncertain date and authorship) which finally cleared up the Trinity business for good and all in a drumming storm of intolerant nonsense, it had practically become a synthesis of all the chief religious cults of that mentally festering age.

The Catholic Church emerged from these formative centuries as an organization of very considerable tenacity, but intellectually it was already the most extraordinary jumble of absurdities and incompatibilities that has ever exercised and perplexed the human intelligence. It accumulated accretions like a caddis worm. Still—though now with more deliberation—it assimilates. At a very early stage it developed sexual obsessions unknown to its cognate Judaism. The Virgin Birth began to worry its usually celibate theologians. Jesus on one occasion (Matthew xx, 47-50) had very definitely denied any religious importance to his mother, but with the taking-over of Isis and the Infant Horus, as the Virgin and Child, this was disregarded. The Virgin became a divine queen, very beautiful and adorable. St. Ignatius Loyola, contemptuous of the earthly attractions he had found unsatisfactory, vowed himself her Knight, and believed there was a mutual devotion. That the intenser religious succumb very readily to the suggestions of such phrases as "The Bride of Christ," one can find ample evidence for in the vast literature of the Christian mystics. It became necessary to sublimate the Virgin, the attractive Queen of Heaven. She had to be made "sinless" and born without "sin." So the theologians excogitated a "sinless" begetting for her. It is difficult to tell these things without a touch of derision. The doctrine of the Immaculate Conception emerged from their meditations. It was mainly a Spanish product, and there is a monument to the Immaculate Conception outside the Alcazar in Seville. It is perfectly decent; it is a grouping of the divines, thinkers and spiritual heroes, grave and dignified figures, who contributed to the perfection of this profound discovery. For centuries, however, this Immaculate Conception was not a matter of faith. It was made so by a bull of Pope Pius IX as recently as 1854. There was a great assembly of bishops and dignitaries in Rome from all parts of the world, a great gathering of adult men robed very beautifully and carrying themselves very seriously. A happy sense of a great consummation pervaded them. And now all good Catholics must believe in the Immaculate Conception of the Virgin Mary, though what it is they think they are believing in I cannot imagine.

And so, century by century, the great fabric of the faith goes on accumulating. It has become a sort of Cumberland Market of religious notions.[1] There is something from everywhere in it and, wherein lies its chief attractiveness, something for everybody. No single mind can cover that mighty mental jumble sale in its entirety, so that anyone willing to be converted has no difficulty in ignoring the less congenial articles of the collection. You will, for example, find the sternest condemnation of socialism, no Catholic can be a Socialist, and then you will find that the author of the com-

[1] For a frank Catholic admission of this, see *Note* 13A.

pletest forecast of communism, commissars and all that, Sir Thomas More, has been canonized as a saint.

The organization of the Church, with its confessional and its spiritual direction, facilitates this fragmentary approach to faith in every possible way. The convert is invited and trained to help in his own subjugation. He is implored to pray for light. He must bury his sense of humor. These, he is told, are serious matters. A hearty laugh at the metaphors of relationship in the triplex composition of the divinity would shatter the whole process. Derision is the deadly enemy of Catholicism; it drives it to indignant persecution, indignant silence or indignant flight, according to the exigencies of the situation.

Christianity picked up the Holy Trinity, it would seem, in the second century, and very manifestly from Alexandria. By that time Alexandria far more than Jerusalem had become the spiritual home of Christianity. Neither St. Paul nor Jesus insisted upon the fundamental importance of right views about the Mystery of the Trinity to their followers. To say the least of it, it was inconsiderate of them to leave it to the author of the Athanasian creed, centuries later, to formulate in terms of the now long-abandoned metaphysics of Alexandria, "The Catholic faith, which except a man believe faithfully he *cannot* be saved." Did Matthew know? Did Peter understand? It leaves one anxious about the ultimate fate even of St. Paul himself.

Why do intelligent people accept this strange heap of mental corruption as a religion and a rule of life? That question will bring us back to that reorientation of the human mind, and that conflict between the actuality of the present and the accumulating reality of the future, to which

I have devoted § 9. They accept it because it is there before them and because it existed long before they did. They grew up to it and even if they were not actually born and bred Catholics, they saw it everywhere taken for granted and treated with respect, cathedrals and shrines, saints and martyrs, in art, in literature, in history, in the world about them. There is no reasoning in a stained-glass window, but there is an immense amount of conviction. To turn from the menaces of stark reality to established religion is to be immediately reassured. To turn from active, questioning minds to the company of the faithful is inexpressibly comforting. And with that you get prescription and direction for all the main issues of life. The Church, the faithful about one, a vast volume of literature and history, agree in saying: "Don't trouble. You are all right. Do as we do and all will be well." At times I have tried to imagine what such a natural born scoffer and rebel as Mr. Hilaire Belloc, whose mental processes have always interested and distressed me, thinks at Mass. But that is just when he suspends all thinking. *Credo quia absurdum,* I suspect is the note of it, a triumphant revolt against his own intelligence. He became a scoffer and rebel against liberalism and scientific revelation because he resented their compelling convincingness. Any fool, he felt, could believe that.

And it is equally easy to understand the attraction of the Catholic Church to those outside but within the influence of the fold. They are already half converts. They "go over" without the slightest examination of the fundamental absurdities of the faith. Conviction comes after a discussion of the Apostolic Succession and the validity of the Protestant Orders. Such things are deliberated very gravely. With a

## CHRISTENDOM

sense of enhanced importance, the convert takes to fish on Fridays, is received, attends Mass, feels unutterable things. Unutterable even to himself. It is all so tremendously established. Quiescence, spiritual peace ensues. Until the anxiety of the times takes hold of these refugees from fact, they will not recognize the element of malignity in the activities of this great organization to which they are clinging. Even then they will feel the utmost reluctance in leaving go. It is their last protection against that terrifying readjustment to creative reality, which would make them responsible adults in this world of limitless danger, limitless difficulty and limitless possibility.

Fantastic, defiantly absurd as this vast pile of the Faith becomes to anyone who dares to go into it and question it fearlessly, it is far less fantastic than the actual organization of the Church. Its central control rests with a close corporation of priests, mainly Italians, the cardinals, who with scarcely a break have elected a continuity of Italian Popes for the last three centuries. Spiritually Italians must be a very superior people.

In the Vatican, in entirely unveracious succession to St. Peter, sustained by a handsome subsidy from the Fascist government and the less reliable contributions of the faithful at large, the Holy Father, in the measure of his intelligence and the quality of his advisers, keeps his court and steers the Church through the pitfalls of this world. He has had the medieval education of a priest; his advisers have worn the mental blinkers of the devout, and just as far as they dare, they influence the political life of the world, according to their limitations and prejudices. In all the democracies the "Catholic vote" obeys the tortuous wisdom of these scheming old anachronisms. Here tyrannies are blessed and here revolts are fomented. The devout in France or Britain, for example, must support the Franco pronunciamento to the infinite injury of their own countries.

Joseph McCabe in his *History of the Popes* tells the story of the Papacy with a certain bitter accuracy and an ample citation of authorities. The Catholic reader will, I know, feel that my recommendation of that outspoken book is in the worst possible taste. But let me nevertheless urge it upon his attention. It will trouble his mind, but it will purge it. But if he asks his co-religionists questions about it, they will make him feel as if he were making rude noises.

When we try to estimate the role the Church is now playing in mundane affairs we have to realize that on earth it has no definite objective at all. It is a vast, self-protective organization which seeks merely to exist and if possible spread. Its friends are those who support and serve it; its enemies—and its enmity has the unrelenting quality of an instinct—are those who have thwarted, controlled and suppressed it. It is against Soviet Russia, against every Protestant system, against every country which insists upon secular education; it is on the side of every government, however corrupt and evil, which attends Mass and makes the sign of the cross. Its real objectives, it alleges, lie in another world. In some strange existence outside time and space the reckoning will be made, and those who have swallowed the Athanasian metaphysics, taken the advice of their priests, and performed all their religious duties, will enjoy heaven, and those who have fallen short will pass to heaven through a state called purgatory or descend into hell forever, according to the enormity of their disrespect. Bolsheviks, I assume, will *all* go to hell.

In the past it was the custom of the Church to suggest that the sufferings in hell and purgatory were essentially physical tortures, and simple folk were given pictures of the damned being burnt in flaming bowls, tormented by red-hot pincers, racked and maltreated very richly and variously. The state of bliss was less fully particularized. Nowadays one hears remarkably little of either the upper or lower aspect of the future state. Yet why is there no copious and attractive literature upon the subject? Why are there no speculative anticipations? Why have Catholic poets recoiled? It should be a most fascinating preoccupation to imagine that unearthly loveliness ahead. There are not even impostors to offer us dreams and visions. No one has ever produced a plausible page from a celestial Baedeker. Even Bunyan's *Pilgrim's Progress* stops short at the gates of the Celestial City. We are left to imagine "these endless Sabbaths the blessed ones see." There is the Book of Revelation indeed, but who except cranks and lunatics reads the Book of Revelation? And that, after all, is symbolic prophecy and not to be mistaken for a picture of reality. The fact of it is that the majority of Christians are not even reasonably curious about the future life, and they are not curious because they have no more positive belief in it than I have. They are Christians because it is the most convenient and agreeable pattern of life for them, and for no other reason whatever.

And yet the Church is something more than a picturesque and reassuring frame for an everyday mode of living. It provides that, just as it provides dispensations, annulments of marriages for the wealthy, titles, blessings, missions, festivals and displays, but such things are by the way. It exists primarily for itself. It is always anticipating and warding off dangers and occasionally it counter-attacks. There is an incessancy in its self-preserving activities, and in this present phase of world crisis it is encouraging much partisan activity.

There comes to hand as I write a book, *Crisis for Christianity* by William Teeling, which summarizes very clearly the ideas of a Catholic reaction and recovery that are stirring the imaginations of the more active faithful. I do not know who William Teeling is. His title page supplies no information beyond his bare name; he has written at least one other book, *The Pope in Politics;* but he seems to have met and discussed affairs with most of the leading Catholics in Europe; and I understand that that very peculiar body, the British Council, which spends £100,000 a year in endearing England to foreigners by sending them carefully chosen, if occasionally highly unrepresentative, samples of British thought and behavior to lecture and talk to them, has availed itself of his services. So that his book gives us not only the present Catholic outlook, but one at least of the many faces the now highly diplomatic and incalculable British Empire turns to the world.

The first thing to remark about this book is that it completely ignores the existence of any modern, scientific picture of the world. So far as I am able to judge, this is a real and not a deliberate ignorance. Mr. Teeling was probably educated in a Catholic atmosphere from which such knowledge is excluded. He seems to have no idea of the Good Life except in what survives today of Christendom,

*White* Christianity that is to say, finding its completest embodiment in the Roman Catholic Church. Regardless of the foreign missions, he fears that Christ may "desert Europe" and leave it "to be completely overrun by the Yellow Races or the Black or the Communists and to pass through horrors undreamt of even today." The most Christian countries of Europe now, he says, are "Franco's Spain, Catholic Belgium and God-fearing Britain." Mrs. Nesta Webster, to whose mentality I have devoted a Note at the end of this book (*Note* 12c), could not have a livelier horror of Jews and Russia. Outside the Christian pale there is one single movement to which he turns with a certain hope and kindliness, and there I think he is probably giving us a fair reflection of the Vatican-centered mentality. He has met and discussed matters, it is to be noted, with the present Pope. He seems to be a fair sample of how Catholics think.

He writes: "No matter what we may think of the Nazi leaders, or the methods they employ, they are at least instilling into the nation as a whole, and not only into those who might be their willing converts in a free country, a desire to help the maimed, to support one's neighbors, to work and live clearly, such as no democratic country is able to show. The democratic governments pay only lip service to much that is Christian, and they scarcely ever try to enforce it, while the Trade Unions and other socialist groups in this country" (i.e., Britain) "encourage, as indeed do some of the less-thoughtful Conservative die-hards, a form of class warfare which Christianity can never tolerate.

"My own feelings are all in favor of a free democracy giving the opportunity to lead a Christian life, seeing that a willing Christian is worth more to God than an unwilling one. But if the democrats do not respond, and under the cloak of freedom carry on a most un-Christian life, can we expect that God should favor them, rather than a disciplined body that at least is practicing some of the teachings of the Sermon on the Mount?"

That is how the Church wishes to see the Nazis today. Our exponent ignores the implacable resolution with which the education of the young is being wrested from the Catholic teachers in favor of Wotan, and the bulk of this edifying book is a discussion of the possibilities of a sympathetic swamping of this Nazi movement by the incorporation of more and more Catholics into the Reich so that at last it will be possible to chip off the flapping ends of the swastika and restore the cross. It is all set out very attractively. The curious reader can learn how Dollfüss on "Great Catholic Day" (Sept. 11th, 1933) inaugurated the first German Corporative Christian State, and less explicitly how he stamped down socialism and labor. It was Dollfüss who betrayed and destroyed the radical republic that had ruled in Austria from the end of the War. It was he who stood behind Major Fey's smashing-up of the workmen's dwellings that had been the pride of the socialist regime in Vienna (Feb. 1934). This was not only a frankly uncivilized act but a piece of political folly.[1]

It left him face to face with the Nazis. They assassinated him in July 1934, but the Catholic Corporative movement went on less confidently under Schuschnigg, until the forcible realization of the Anschluss in 1938 by the Nazi army made Austria an integral part of the Reich.

Ultimately Mr. Teeling thinks Nazi Germany will have

[1] John Gunther's *Inside Europe* is particularly good on this.

an indigestion of Catholics. That is his hope. Large parts of Bavaria, Baden and possibly Württemberg and the Rhineland, are to break away and join up with Austria. Communism may gain control in Italy—Mr. Teeling throws that out quite abruptly and gives no reason for his assumption—and then the Vatican will have to make Vienna its headquarters. Nazism and Fascism will be at a discount, and the Authoritarian State, founded on the suggestions of the Papal Encyclical *Quadragesimo Anno* (Pius XI, 1931) for a corporative society will be installed in Vienna, with the Emperor Otto at its head and the Pope near by.

There you have the sort of thing the energetic young Catholics of today can imagine; the sort of thing the present "God-fearing" British government is unobtrusively subsidizing and spreading about, to the ultimate confusion of all Jews, atheists, men of science, Bolsheviks, Russians (but see the *Note* 12c on Mrs. Nesta Webster.) . . .

So much for the Catholic contribution to human adjustment today.

We are too apt to forget the narrow educational limitations of those who figure as wise, unquestionable leaders of men. Everywhere that applies, we live in a medley of ignorant systems, but it is the Catholic culture I am now discussing. It is a common tendency in our minds to believe that what we know clearly is also known clearly to other people. We are all too apt to believe that these dignified directors of human consciences know and understand the body of modern knowledge, that they have studied, judged it and rejected it.

But these Catholic prelates, so imposing in their triple crowns and miters and epicene garments, are in fact extremely ignorant men, not only by virtue of the narrow specialization of their initial education, but also by the incessant activities of service and ceremony that have occupied them since. They can have read few books, they can have had no opportunities of thinking freely. They are not nearly the cynical rogues so many non-Catholics think them; most of them are trying most earnestly to do right by the dim and dwindling oil-lamps inside their brains. They are quite ready to believe Mr. Belloc when he tells them, with that buoyant assurance of his, that Darwin was inspired by the ambition to abolish God in the universe. That fits in completely with their prepossessions. Why should they seek further? Mentally they live in another universe from ours, and the pity is that materially our universes intersect.

The slovenly, unorganized, intellectual world in which we and they live together, gives them no opportunity of grasping modern ideas without an impossible expenditure of perplexing inquiry. And to set against that we must remember that their world of theological elaborations remains an unmapped jungle to the unbeliever. They may have something to say to us but we are quite unable to get it, and conversely. The mind of mankind is still like a scattered jigsaw puzzle, bits of knowledge here and bits of knowledge there and no common pattern visible. And until we have something in the nature of that permanent world encyclopædia I have tried to foreshadow, so matters must remain. That revival of the Holy Roman Empire under the Emperor Otto, which strikes a realistic modern intelligence as fantastically absurd, presents itself to the Vatican intelligence in the guise of sober and subtle statecraft.

It is not necessary for us to wait for the return of the Holy Roman Empire to appreciate the nature of the Roman Catholic Christian State. In Eire (formerly Southern Ireland) and in Spain, the Church rules and we can watch it in operation. Franco's Spain is still too busy cleaning up the Republican Opposition, by shootings, expulsions and proscriptions, to develop the Christian life in its complete beauty, but in Ireland, Catholicism has been in control for some years.

A stringent censorship of books and publications and a fairly complete control of education have produced a first crop of young men, as blankly ignorant of the modern world as though they had been born in the thirteenth century, mentally concentrated upon the idea of bringing the Protestant North under Catholic control in the sacred name of national unity. That tension of the young men to which so much social disturbance is due seems to be increasing. There has been a steady flow of emigrants to Great Britain, and recently there have been a number of bomb outrages designed to terrorize the British government into an abandonment of Northern Ireland. These patriotic zealots set about their business in a vein of pious devotion. They take Mass and purify their souls by confession—of everything but the particular enterprise they have in hand. And if the British police deal sternly with these foolish, misguided youngsters, all Catholic Ireland will set up a great outcry, possibly with more and better bombing, to avenge or release this new crop of national martyrs.

The future of Ireland is incalculable. Hopeful Irishmen abroad have indulged in dreams of a restless and independent-minded people tiring of priests, piety and patriotism and returning presently as an animating influence to world civilization. But how can these young men get the idea of that? We may perhaps find sounder intimations of Ireland's future in the experiences of the Catholic South American States. A people which learns little forgets nothing, and the Church in Eire may be trusted to see to it that the young men of Ireland learn little and so sustain their tradition that inveterate animosities are dignified and desirable. The probabilities seem to point to murderous faction fighting, with Northern Ireland and England always to fall back upon in phases of comparative unity. There is a close temperamental kinship between the Irish and the Spanish, and the history of South America has already produced a series of bosses and pronunciamentos, vindictive massacres and pitiless wars.

Never has there been such heroic, cruel, senseless warfare as those little Christian hells in South America have known. Paraguay under Solano Lopez fought on until its population was reduced from 1,300,000 to under a quarter of a million. Regiments were made up of boys between twelve and fifteen, and women were enrolled to carry ammunition and stores. When these women could keep up no longer, they were either left to die by the roadside or, if there was any chance of their falling into the enemy's hands and yielding information, butchered out of hand. No doubt many a wretched young conscript rebelled against his lot, but what could he do? He might hope for a change of leaders. He had no other ideas. It was impossible for him to have other ideas.

The Roman Catholic Church, that clumsy system of frustrations, that strange compendium of ancient traditions and habit systems, since it lies in the closest entanglement with the intellectual life of the Western world and still holds many millions in its grip, is certainly the most formidable single antagonist in the way of human readjustment to the dangers and frustration that now close in upon us all.

## 14

## WHAT IS PROTESTANTISM?

THE CONFLICT OF JUDAISM and anti-Judaism is a tragedy involving the misery and destruction of at most a few million people, and were it not that the abolition of distance has made every one of us his brother's keeper, it would be an incident of secondary importance in the general collapse of civilization that is now going on. But the struggle of Christianity to maintain its present ascendancy affects the larger part of the human race. The Roman Catholic Church is the most highly organized and efficient embodiment of Christian teaching, the Orthodox Churches of Greece, Serbia, Russia and the like are relatively negligible systems of ceremony and superstition, the British Imperial culture it will be more convenient to consider later, and the next group of world forces to which we must direct our attention is the Protestantisms, that series of movements and organizations which has arisen through the incapacity or unwillingness of people to accept this or that outstanding incredibility of the Catholic faith.

They protested. But for the most part they did not protest outright against the ensemble of Church beliefs. That would have been too awful for them. The earlier reaction was to discover some incompatibility between the Bible and

## WHAT IS PROTESTANTISM?

the practice and teaching of the Church. The courage of the Protestant has grown by degrees. None of these earlier doubters were capable of facing, even in their secret hearts, the terrific isolation of denying Christianity. Such a denial was almost unthinkable in Christendom for those born within the pale, and they did not think it. For reasons we made plain in the preceding section, when we asked why it is that fairly well-educated people cannot merely remain but become Roman Catholics, these early dissentients clung quite desperately to the assertion of their essential orthodoxy.

A convergence of mechanical inventions occurred in the sixteenth century to strengthen the Book against the priest; paper in sheets of a uniform size replaced parchment, and the rapid multiplication of books by printing from movable type became possible. Suddenly Europe was sprayed with Bibles and vernacular translations of the Bible, and the Church found itself assailed by a variety of new Protestantisms that steadily gathered strength and enterprise. Men brooded dubiously over the inspired word. All the Protestants began as "reformers," and their original protests were the distressful cries of honest men, who were—as I have noted in an earlier section—usually priests.

But though the Church monopolized education, ruled men's minds, sanctioned and condemned conduct, adjudicated on political claims, preached crusades, excommunicated, put states under interdicts, and held an ever increasing accumulation of land and wealth, it had never secured a physical grip upon the secular arm. It trusted for obedience to the spiritual fears it could arouse and the civil inconveniences it could cause. It could turn state against state and subjects against their rulers. It could dissolve allegiances. In an illiterate world this gave it an effective security. Many monarchs and princes lived in a state of uneasy resentment against the restrictions imposed upon their conduct. There was a continual struggle going on over such things as the appointment of bishops, the restriction of gifts and bequests to the Church, the taxation of its accumulating property. These lords and princes struggled and lived and died, but the Church had a massive continuity. Sooner or later it recovered its concessions and advanced to further aggrandizements. So long, that is, as its moral power, its grip upon the minds and consciences of the people, remained.

It could bluff its way through many scandals and abuses so long as faith was unimpaired. But these honest doubters and critics, with their arguments and proofs, gave a novel strength to the recalcitrance of the princes. Before, they had been recalcitrant like naughty boys, there had been fear and the possibility of repentance behind their outrages, but now they began to behave like youths growing up and discovering flaws and weaknesses in the character of the governess that hitherto even in their disobedience they had respected. They seized very gladly upon this new destructive criticism of the doctrines of the Church. They gave the reformers their protection and ample opportunity to spread their doctrines. So that a thinly concealed desire for autonomy and the confiscation of the vast estates of the Church, mingled very remarkably with honest protestations in the Protestant Reformation.

All this is a matter of history. We need not recapitulate the process by which the new Protestant States that detached themselves from Rome sought first to utilize and then to limit this process of protesting and questioning, of which

## WHAT IS PROTESTANTISM?

they had made such good use, by setting up government-controlled Established Churches. Nor need we do more than glance at the way in which Peter the Great took a leaf from the English Establishment and applied the same process of nationalization to the Orthodox Church in Russia. These Protestant State Churches play a diminishing role in the present drama of human affairs. What is of greater interest for the purposes of our present inquiry is the inability of any of these would-be-religious settlements, as reading, writing and controversy spread, to arrest the progressive release of the human intelligence.

The implementing of the Bible by printing had two divergent results. The most conspicuous at first was a definite return towards the spirit of Old Testament Judaism. The Old Testament is the larger, more various and intriguing part of the Word. One theme in it, which appealed more to the reformers and thoughtful subjects generally than to the princes, was the Calvinistic theme, the assertion of a stern Theocracy, the rebuking and warning of kings by prophets, a republicanism under God. The other, politically more agreeable to the established rulers, attached less importance to predestination and more to the good works that came naturally from the Christian monarch. According to the former doctrine he might fail to be one of the elect and be denounced and disobeyed in this life and damned forever in the next, however amiable his behavior. According to the Lutheran alternative he justified himself by the inevitable rightness of his works.

Here we cannot enlarge on these attempts to adjust the new Bible Christianity to the needs of that period. But one very natural mental twist may be noted, and that was the widespread disposition of the Protestant Christians to identify themselves with the Chosen People, either mystically or physically. It would need a small encyclopædia to recapitulate the writers, movements and societies that have sought to prove some magical migration of the "Lost Ten Tribes" to Western Europe. There are British Israelites of that persuasion today. Such a jungle of absurdities it is, as could only flourish in an ill-instructed world. But one curious variant upon this craving to be an elite with specific divine favor we shall have to consider when we come to estimate the value of the Nazi movement in the complication of human destiny. . . .

The reversion of large parts of Christendom to Bibliolatry and the Chosen People idea was however only the first and most immediate result of the invention of printed books. Many accepted the authority and read and believed. But some read and thought and compared as they read. Gathering momentum more slowly was a new skepticism, which began to question the divinity of the Bible itself.

The doctrine of the Trinity was on the whole one of the less fortunate acquisitions of the Catholic Church. It has always given trouble from the days of the Arian heresy onward. It gave Charlemagne an excuse for breaking with Greek orthodoxy on the profoundly important point whether the Holy Ghost proceeds from the Father only or from the Father and the Son. Arian and Trinitarian, Latin and Greek—the history of their wars was written in the blood of millions. With the increase of questioning in Christendom, that triplex divinity began presently not merely to untwist but to lose its second and third strands altogether.

Men dared presently to call themselves Unitarian, bowing politely but distantly to the Biblical record.

Then came another step. A fashion of skepticism spread among the European nobility and gentry in the seventeenth and eighteenth centuries; bold spirits encouraged each other to the pitch of doubting and ridiculing the Bible altogether. They became naughtily wicked about it. They were deists. There were soon enough of them to live in easy understanding with each other. Voltaire and Gibbon typify their quality. But atheism still remained a rather shocking extravagance. Only temerarious individuals professed so extreme a lack of belief, and usually it was associated with defiant blasphemies and a general pretension to extreme depravity. By this note of defiance in their excesses, these eighteenth-century atheists betrayed a lingering belief in the God they had denied. It was the ideas of God and good not only in the world about them but in themselves that they fought down.

The bright young people who gathered about Sir Francis Dashwood at Medmenham Priory set out to be terrible fellows with their Hell Fire Club and their Black Masses, but how could one get the slightest thrill out of a Black Mass unless one had a lingering awe of the Mass itself? Without that much belief a Black Mass is an inane burlesque of nothing in particular.

It is only in our own time that Protestantism, the progressive etching away of belief by inquiry, has reached its natural finality in complete, untroubled disbelief in superhuman authority. Even now many atheists prevaricate. If the word "God" means anything at all, it means a powerful being sufficiently anthropomorphic to have reciprocal relations with the individual man. A God who is not a personality is a contradiction in terms. But because of the ribald and ungenteel associations of the word "atheist," a great number of atheistic thinkers and teachers and writers have clung ambiguously to the entirely deflated name of "God." God, they say, is the Absolute, he is a force not ourselves making for righteousness, he is the whisper of conscience, he is the brainless Thinker responsible for the mathematical order of the world, he is immanence. These are mere subterfuges, God-shaped vacuums.

A sort of theism in effect, a theistic feeling at the beginning of life, may be as innate as suckling. The natural and necessary disposition of all immature creatures to believe they are being taken care of, survives and will no doubt survive always. Even if they do not think in theistic terms they will still believe in protection. And throughout the Western world, in Christendom and Islam and Israel, children will be constantly hearing talk of God, so that a father-like divinity becomes the form of this basic feeling. Until a mind is fully adult, it finds great comfort in that ancient personification of a natural but transitory need. And there is still a disposition on the part of unbelieving parents and of teachers who should know better to utilize this craving for dependence in the moral training of their children. Most educational psychologists are convinced that it gives a better result in behavior to teach children that the right thing should be done, not because of an all-seeing eye or a loving Father in Heaven, but because it is simply just that—the right thing to do. Innumerable Confucians and Buddhists have lived

## WHAT IS PROTESTANTISM? 141

noble and beautiful lives without the assistance of an unseen Inspector.

Protestantism carried on to its end is a complete acceptance of the limitless, impartial and continually more wonderful universe that scientific inquiry is illuminating for us; that is to say, it culminates in atheism without qualification. Its final stage is a world of grown men, free from superstitious fear and free equally from belief in any guidance of the world that can relieve them from responsibility for the shortcomings and failures of our race.

## 15

### THE NAZI RELIGION

WE COME NOW TO the Nazi movement, which is, in its possibilities of destruction, the most urgent challenge the human mind and will have ever had to face. Nazi Germany may well bring down conclusive disaster on our species. Yet its intellectual content is naive, and its sudden extreme importance the result of a convergence of accidents. A people almost stupidly warlike, led by a maniac, threatens the world and holds in its hands all the exaggerated powers of destruction modern science and invention have created.

It is plain that the Fuehrer is insane; he shows all the symptoms of a recognized form of sex mania, the jealous fear and hate of the great raping black man—who in his case becomes the Jew. Since in his case his obsession endangers the lives of people about him, he should be certified and put under restraint. But insanity has its advantages as well as its handicaps. It involves an abnormal concentration of purpose and nervous energy. In its phase of mania it abolishes or at least defers fatigue and sustains long spells of sleepless vigilance and penetrating distrust far beyond the compass of the normal man. These qualities alone never made any man the leader of a mighty nation. Hitler's insanity would have had little effect upon the world if it had

## THE NAZI RELIGION

not slotted very easily into certain essential needs of the German situation. But for that he might be shouting, frothing and orating in a madhouse at the present time. But it happened that he supplied just the inflexible spearhead, the inhuman pertinacity, required to give extreme expression to the feelings of a humiliated and outrageously treated people.

The Nazi movement, or something essentially like it, was inevitable. Had there been no Hitler, or were Hitler to vanish tomorrow, Germany would still be the problem sister among the European states, the embittered and crazy sister clutching the high explosive bomb.

The Nazi movement was inevitable because she had a greater surplus of young people without reasonable hope of life than any other country in the world. They had no colonies to go to, no great business enterprises to develop; no employment of any sort. There you have the primary condition for a desperate outbreak. If you want the state of mind of pre-Nazi Germany compactly rendered, read Hans Fallada's *Little Man, What Now?* That post-war generation grew up to explode and it has exploded. What else could have happened?

In § 12 the conditions under which social order may degenerate into phases of suspicion, persecution, and plunder have been discussed. Post-war Germany displayed these conditions to an exaggerated degree. A new regime should have its own new education to explain itself to the community, but the staggering liberal Republican Germany of the twenties carried on without any revolution in its schools and colleges. They had become a great means of patriotic consolidation under the Hohenzollern regime, they had been purged and vetted for a third of a century to that end, and now they were hard at work establishing in the minds of a new generation the innocence of Germany for the war and the conviction that she had never been defeated; she had been cheated and betrayed. She was suffering bitterly through no fault of her own. The teachers mined the democratic republic. Everything was ripe for an outbreak of hysterical patriotism and a great pogrom before Hitler became of the slightest importance.

And here another factor in the mentality of that dominating section of the German peoples which we may call Nordic-conscious came into play. Much of it was only less anti-Catholic than it was anti-Jewish. Its mentality had been framed upon the Lutheran interpretation of the Bible, and with a certain acceptable reversal it was possible to apply the conception of a Chosen People to the Germanic world. The Nazis took that over in one magnificent plagiarism. The Slav Prussians, the Alpine Bavarians, the *mélange* of Gothic and Celtic peoples in the Rhineland, discovered that they were one single, pure race of beautiful blonds. They saw through their mirrors to the inner truth of themselves. They knew that in spite of appearances they had lovely, pure, blond souls. They turned upon the Jews and all foreigners with the completest paraphrase of the old Bible nationalism. And, wiser in their generation than the post-war liberal Republic, they have seized upon the schools and universities, and are doing their best to mold the mentality of the entire Reich to this fundamentally Biblical idea of a militant Chosen People—Germanized.

Explicitly the new teaching retranslates Jehovah as Wotan, the old Kaiser's *unser alter Gott,* and flouts the most elementary concepts of Christianity. But it is impossible to estimate with what consistency this new religion of heroic combat is being imposed upon the youth of the Reich. Variations in statement may set the brighter ones thinking. All the books have not been burnt. We do not know how much of social democracy remains beneath the Nazified surface. We do not know how much counter-propaganda is going on in the outwardly submissive and still tolerated Protestant and Roman Catholic congregations.

I have cited Mr. William Teeling to show the Roman Catholic expectation of a German return to the faith, but I doubt whether he fully realizes the relentless vigor of the educational drive of the new religion. In Austria just as much as in Germany they are turning the children against parent and priest. Mr. Teeling, I think, counts his Catholics before they are hatched. He would be wiser to count them after they are educated. The complete de-Christianization of the entire Reich, of southern as of northern Germany, is, I think, the greater probability.[1]

But that involves no release of German thought; it is only a relapse into organized, relentless barbarism. Science in Germany has been silenced completely. There is no free scientific opinion any more. What remains of German science is enslaved to produce either secret discoveries of military importance or sustain the crazy ethnology of race superiority. But if research in non-German countries is forced, barbarism for barbarism, to adopt a reciprocal protective secrecy, it may not be long before Germany realizes a decline in her technical efficiency. She may cease to make discoveries herself and she may be able no longer to borrow them from abroad and develop them for her own purposes. This may

[1] See *School for Barbarians* by Erika Mann (1939).

move her to some loosening of the gag on her laboratories and an attempt to re-open communications with the alien world outside. And that again may undermine that still very unstable Wotan.

The problem of what will happen in Germany is the major problem of our immediate future. If the Nazi process continues upon its present lines, then all the world must be given over to the servitude of war preparation, at least until Nazi Germany ceases to exist. So far, Germany has conquered the earth already. The demonstration of the impossibility of independent sovereign states under modern conditions is complete. This finishes it. The declared Nazi objective is to create a unanimous, belligerent Germany, a bloodthirsty nation, entirely tough and ruthless, resolved to use any weapons and any methods, however monstrous and destructive, in its march to world dominion. It will fight and conquer, or blow the world to pieces.

How will that drive to destruction end? It is possible but highly improbable that this desperate adventure may succeed, and the whole world, or what is left of it, may cower at last at the feet of Wotan's Chosen People, its masters. Or that after a world storm of war, more horrible than any war has ever been, Germany may be defeated and stamped out by victors become at last as ruthless as their enemies. Or as a third possibility; something may occur within Germany to shake the Nazi solidarity. Many accidents are possible. Mental forces at present unrevealed may appear. All German thought is not in concentration camps. Individuals may die, new groupings may occur, resolution may falter at the eleventh hour. Every month that this tension endures without an actual explosion, the search for escape from

## THE NAZI RELIGION

Armageddon will become more intelligent both within and without Germany. The magnitude of the still impending danger will help more and more people to realize the magnitude of the reconstruction needed to restore safety and hope to mankind. Which means, *inter alia,* restoring security, hope and ample scope for energetic activities, to the stifled youth of Germany—from whose exploited frustrations all this trouble has arisen.

Before we leave this vital question of the German outlook, it may be well to note one sinister possibility in contemporary thought. Because of the peculiar filthiness and malignity of the Nazi concentration camps, because of the sheer horror of the stories told by the more or less broken creatures who have escaped from them, there is a widespread disposition to assert that Germans are particularly cruel; that they are indeed a specially evil-spirited variety of human being. Old stories of atrocities are being revived. Now this is to concede the Nazi claims to be a unique people. We cannot have it both ways, and, if we argue, as we have done in the preceding sections, that the Germans are not the pure blond Chosen People they imagine themselves to be, but a *mélange* of Slav, Celtic, Gothic and Alpine elements with only a language to bind them together, then we cannot also entertain this idea of a specific sadistic streak in Germans.

Yet when we compare the evidence of those who have been interned in various countries, we find a general agreement in one respect, in regard to the attitude of the minor officials towards the prisoners, which at the first glance does seem to justify this particular charge against the Germans. There is a consensus of evidence by those who have been there, that in British and Russian prisons the attitude of the guard, the warder, the turnkey and so forth is generally sympathetic to his charges. Fellow feeling is his quality. He regrets his instructions and does his best to mitigate them. At times he may lose his temper or dislike and bully someone, but that is an individual lapse. But his German equivalent, there is no doubt of it, does his tortures with zest, hates his charges as though they were loathsome animals, and is ingenious in devising new pains and abasements and suffering for them. It is important that we should make up our minds about the real nature of this difference. If it is innate, then biologically it would be an excellent thing to kill all Germans.

But most of us who have known and seen Germans intimately have found them as humane and helpful as most people. They are generally more law-abiding than the Irish or the English. They like to be relieved of the dangers and troubles of responsibility by explicit directions. That may be a habit of mind due to a persuasion that this is a dangerous world with which it is unwise to take liberties, and it is quite compatible with these cruelties. The position of the Germans in Central Europe has always exposed them to an exceptional imminence of warfare. The country has been overrun time after time by alien armies. Plunder and rapine have flowed over the land. The German-speakers lived for the most part in a great plain, they had no mountains in which they could hide. It was only by screwing themselves up to fighting pitch and facing all comers, that the divided German states were able to maintain themselves at all. They were called upon by their circumstances to be tougher fighters than any other Europeans.

Toughness therefore is as much in the German tradition as it was, for other reasons, in the Spartan. They had to despise fear and pain in themselves, and that for most human beings means despising fear and pain in others. The Nazi is not a born tough. If he were changed at birth and put among gentle, fearless people, he would not be a tough at all. He is a being innately as gentle as you and I, only he is inspired by an hysterical desire to be utterly tough. He refuses to give way to the horror of other people's torments, because from doing that it is only a step to giving way to pain and fear himself. And, attacking his own shrinking and disgust, he goes out of his way in a sort of desperation, to devise and inflict ruthless, disgusting and intolerable things on the recalcitrants, the evil-doers, the detected conspirators —and we must remember that he has been made to believe them that—committed to him for reformation. Deliberate cruelty is not a characteristic of limitless strength. Great strength may be heedless and unconsciously cruel, but not ingeniously and appreciatively cruel. It would get no thrill out of it. That is reserved for men and women who are inwardly afraid. It is sensitive people who seek to sustain and fix themselves by outrages.

Here it would take us too far from our main argument to examine other cases of torture and cruelty, the abominations done by Red Indian and Arab women for example, after battles. There is indeed no people on earth against whom some phase of cruelty cannot be brought. The English assume themselves to be a particularly gentle people, and with some truth now. Yet consider the cockshies and bear- and bull-baiting that delighted their ancestors in the past and the extreme savagery of the penal laws at the end of the eighteenth century. There is a strain of cruelty, suppressed or overt, in every human being. It is inseparable from self-assertion and the craving to exercise power. . . .

But enough has been said to qualify this charge of a special German cruelty. Those concentration camps must be forgotten if ever Germany comes to judgment. Vindictive reprisals may be part of the behavior pattern of a patriotic Irish Catholic who knows no better, but not of a civilized man. Let the dead past bury its grievances. They can have no part in the rational reconstruction of human life. . . .

And here, apt to my argument, comes confirmation. Since I wrote the above I have had a talk with a man who has been in a German concentration camp, and he told me of how an official, instructed to give him, for no particular reason, thirty lashes, fell into conversation with him after the second stroke, found out that he had been the editor of an illustrated paper he liked, sat talking journalism, omitted the rest of the prescribed beating, saying only, "I suppose your friend here won't give us away," quite after the Russian or English pattern. The friend was trustworthy. All fellow-prisoners are not trustworthy. One of the minor vilenesses of Dachau is that prisoners are bribed by petty indulgences and payments to report small relaxations of discipline. And many are in such physical misery, craving to smoke, craving for taste of sweetness, that they do.[1]

[1] See Stefan Lorant's *I was Hitler's Prisoner*.

# 16

## TOTALITARIANISM

TOTALITARIANISM IS NO NEW thing in the Western world. It is stated very completely in Hobbes' *Leviathan*. Leviathan is the State into which the individual life is almost completely incorporated. Its will is concentrated on the sovereign who heads the collective monster by right divine. He makes war and peace, he raises up and casts down, he levies taxes as he will. Even while Hobbes was preparing his book for press, England decapitated Leviathan in the person of Charles the First. The practical difficulty of the Corporative State has always been the question who should be the head and how a new head should succeed its predecessor. The High Anglican Church upheld the monarchy and maintained the hereditary principle, but the liberal gentry, the merchants and the tax-paying classes generally, were too much for the state monster.

Except in the case of Franco's Spain and the extinguished Catholic Corporative State of Dollfüss, the heads of the totalitarian states of today are usually sustained by "parties" of a distinctly gangsterish quality. At the cost of mental flexibility and adaptability, the corporate state gains a certain immediate concentration of will. Our problem is to estimate what amount of mischief these obstinately knotted will systems may do with the monstrous weapons of the present time, before they themselves can be undone. It may be irreparable mischief.

The Nazi culture has been weighed in the previous section. Now we turn to its weaker associate, fascism. This is immediately interwoven with the career of one single man, Benito Mussolini. Compared with Hitler he is sane, intelligent and human. He is vain, rhetorical and immensely energetic, with the energy not of morbid concentration but physical abundance. He is what many men would like to be. His career from his early days as a socialist conspirator, when oddly enough he was already nicknamed *il Duce,* to his present supremacy on the crest of middle age, is a fairly open book. It is laced throughout with a thread of the ridiculous. Where Hitler is an unqualified horror, Mussolini often is, as schoolboys say, a bit of an ass, which is much more endearing. Until we remember the castor oil campaign and the poison bombs in Abyssinia and the Lipari Islands, and Amendola and Mateotti and Roselli and the like, he is a lark. But then the lark stops singing. We know absurdities about him from which he cannot escape. We have the researches of the curious and the revelations of intimates. Madame Balabanoff [1] tells a fairly convincing story of his life at Geneva. Mr. G. Megaro [2] gives the particulars of his upbringing among the rebel spirits of the Romagna, quotes relentlessly from his early speeches, and shows with chapter and verse how strenuous have been his efforts to conceal the truth about his early career. That anxious eye on posterity, these absurd and belated efforts to escape the unre-

---

[1] *My Life as a Rebel* (1938).
[2] *Mussolini in the Making* (1938).

lenting pens that pursue him, are naturally pleasing to a writer with a weakness for derision.

But do not let us judge Mussolini only by the writings of his enemies. A more flattering study, written indeed in terms of unrestrained admiration, is *My Autobiography*. It was dictated by the Duce himself at the request of Mr. Richard Washburn Child, if possible a more fulsome hero-worshiper than the autobiographer himself, and it is amusing to compare its evasive flourishes with the relentless documentation of Megaro. If one learns little about the blacksmith father one gets hitherto disregarded particulars about the aristocratic Mussolinis of former days and their armorial bearings and castles and so forth. Anybody on record who was ever called Mussolini seems to have been his ancestor and to have anticipated some or all of his distinctive qualities.[1]

Here we are not concerned either with biography or history except in so far as they throw light on the present world situation, but it is of very great importance in our estimate of the future of fascism to realize that the personal vitality of its creator must now be passing its maximum. He was born in 1883. For some years there has been an increasing appearance of effort and uncertainty in his grandiose gestures. It is as if he felt Italy was slipping away from beneath him. He has manifestly become dependent on the tougher initiatives of Nazi Germany. He is less sure of the Church. Six years ago he was holding up Dollfüss in Austria as a barrier against Hitler. And where is that barrier now? The Nazis look down on him from the Brenner Pass. He is losing face with his own people and his Nazi friends do

[1] See also Professor Salvemini's *The Fascist Dictatorship in Italy* (1928).

little to help him in that matter. A few years ago it was dangerous to talk about him in Italy. Now they are talking.

Can there be a second Duce to follow the first? His high-spirited daughter and his son-in-law, Count Ciano, seem impatient to outdo his Fascist intemperance, but they will scarcely dare to attack and oust him, and it is not in his character to resign. Unless some unanticipated accident removes him from the scene, we shall have, not Giovinezza, but a middle-aged fascism to reckon with from now on.

The Italian situation has several incongruous elements and their relative importance varies continually. The Vatican (*pace* Mr. Teeling and his friends) seems now firmly dug in at Rome. Its relations to fascism have always lacked enthusiasm; it has ideas of its own. In the case of Fascist collapse or national defeat, the monarchy also stands ready to return and save the country. If the monarchy returned, would it be liberal or Catholic totalitarian? And the foreigner knows nothing of the possibilities of social discontent in Italy. Italy is a land peculiarly unfitted to stand the stresses of modern war. She is mostly coast line. She has no coal, and the Apennines are a thousand feet too low for her to have snowfields that would give her irrigation or water power. She can better defend herself against Germany in the Alps than against the sea power of France and Britain.

All these considerations lead towards the same conclusion, that in the probable war tornado of the near future, Italy, if she is not clever enough to keep out of it, will play a secondary and gesticulating role. She may suffer many things. She has not the fixed will, and she cannot afford to have the fixed will, for war, at which the Nazi culture aims. It is Nazi Germany which remains the danger center of mankind.

## 17

### THE BRITISH OLIGARCHY

THE NEXT NETWORK OF thought and behavior we must bring into this reckoning of world forces is the British Empire. British Imperialism, like Roman Catholicism, is a natural aggregation. No man planned it; it discovered itself in being. It is a crowned oligarchy, claiming to be democratic because it uses universal suffrage for election to one of its two Houses of Parliament, and to correct that it has an easily manipulated voting system and a proprietary press dependent on advertisement revenue for the information of its citizens. At no phase in history have the common people played a dominant part in the government of Great Britain, and in every phase the baronial oligarchy has prevailed. It is the tradition and education of this oligarchy which determines the behavior of the Imperial Government and its role in contemporary world affairs.

Runnymede is the typical scene in the pageant of English liberties; Magna Carta documents the fundamental British situation. Magna Carta secures the liberties of the baron and free yeomen of the realm from all the main abuses of unqualified monarchy. It concedes no more rights to the churls and common folk of the land than it does to cats and dogs. About this central picture of the monarch amidst his barons English history groups itself. The king is restive, but his peers are stern. They war with the Scots and the French and they conquer and parcel out Ireland. The Church carries on its habitual struggle for existence, asserts itself, is restrained; it becomes rich and is reformed and plundered. The Crown, with a Tory following and a sympathetic Church, tries to go back upon Magna Carta, asserting its divine right to absolutism, and one king is beheaded and another goes into exile with his family, leaving the oligarchy, with a manageable new dynasty of Hanoverians, in possession. It over-exploits its American colonies and loses them, and it happens upon a greater Empire in the East.

Never once in the proud island story does the will of the common people matter a rap. Occasionally they give trouble; they get rather out of control after the Black Death; and a little later we find them asking quite inconclusively:

> "When Adam delved and Eve span
> Who was then the gentleman?"

They subside into deepening misery with the industrial revolution, and they reappear in the nineteenth century struggling for nothing more than better wages and rather more tolerable living conditions. There was nothing very democratic about British trade unionism—as we have defined democracy in § 6—and hardly more in the Labor Party that derived from it. The British Labor Party has never displayed any ambition to direct the affairs of the Empire. It aspires to nothing of the sort. It acknowledges the class inferiority of the workers and haggles by means of strikes and votes for a more tolerable but admittedly inferior way of living. By diminishing the discomfort of the masses and mitigating and soothing the exasperations caused by excessive business enterprise, it plays a stabilizing role in the existing system. Not only is it utterly absurd to call the British government now or at any time in the past a democratic government, but it flies in the face of manifest facts to deny that it is farther off now from anything that can be recognized as a democracy than it was thirty years ago. The old Liberal Party was liberal in its professions at any rate; the Labor Party is densely conservative. The British masses neither rule nor want to rule. They are politically apathetic. They do not produce outstanding individuals to express their distinctive thoughts or feelings, because they have no distinctive thoughts or feelings to express. Outstanding individuals of humble origin are obliged to fall into more or less easy acquiescence with the ruling system. There is nothing else for them to do. The oligarchy is privileged, it has to be served first at table with everything, office, honors, opportunity, but it is not exclusive, and that is one of the factors in its continued existence.

I do not know of any comprehensive study of the education and training of the British ruling class throughout the ages. The feudal world was limited enough for a lord to get away with very little reading and writing. He had his clerk, his cleric, at his elbow, and he felt he could keep his eye on him. His world was all in sight. Leech, lawyer and priest knew their places and stuck to them. The renascence and the coming of the printed book altered all that. The medieval universities were swarms of poor scholars. The gentleman of the renascence had his tutor at home and went to grammar school and university. The grammar school became the narrowing portals through which the poor scholar had now to pass on his way to the learned professions. The Latin and Greek classics came into the Western world first as a stimulant and then, as the pedagogues watered learning down to scholarship, as a distinctive culture. The British oligarchy of the sixteenth and seventeenth centuries conceived of itself as Roman patricians and was rather ashamed of its illiterate members. It made the grand tour with its tutor, achieved a sort of French and Italian and became artistic and architectural. The apt classical quotation adorned the Parliamentary debates into the middle of the nineteenth century. After that it became infrequent. It was not that the classics were going out of fashion but that the standard of learning was sinking.

Culturally the British oligarchy was at its best in the seventeenth century. It knew what it wanted and how to get it. It managed its estates ably. It built fine houses, it made great progress in agriculture; its younger sons went into trade and spread adventurously into America, India, China. A prolific Protestant clergy supplemented the supply of enterprising young men. Yet a shadow fell upon the outlook with the Hanoverian importation, and Pope's *Dunciad* marked the change. The Goddess Dullness is enthroned:

"And at her fell approach and secret might
Art after art goes out and all is night."

The oligarchy still ruled and flourished materially under that unstimulating dynasty, but it made no further progress mentally; it ceased to be alert and adaptable, it became acquisitive, tenacious and conservative. Because of these quali-

## THE BRITISH OLIGARCHY

ties it presently irritated the thirteen American colonies into separation. The French Revolution took it by surprise. When the French in their turn decapitated their king it was not flattered by the imitation. It was scared. The revolutionary mob, it realized, was something different from the Ironsides. The Ironsides sang hymns and were sternly respectable. These people from Marseilles sang a much more alarming song.

The deterioration of an education is usually a complicated process. The mere fact that it is materially successful makes for uncritical contentment, and discredits change. Teaching falls into the hands of sound, orthodox, unenterprising men. It becomes humdrum. Interest shifts to the greater reality of the playing fields. The history of British education—of the education of the oligarchy, that is to say, for popular education had hardly begun—from 1760 to 1860 is a history of resistance to change and steady deterioration.

The nineteenth-century British gentry had nothing like the full-bodied classical education of the preceding centuries; they had only the pedagogic vestiges of that education. Mathematical studies had been introduced, but they were as stylistic and useless as the pedants could make them. By the middle of the nineteenth century the self-complacency of the British governing classes was being protected educationally not only from the subversive ideas of the French Encyclopædists and the French Revolution, but also from that more fundamental upheaval which was making biological science the key to a modernized mentality. A dwindling section of the upper classes could read French still; there was an attractive breadth in the French novel that the domestic fiction of the period did not display; but Voltaire and Gibbon were passing out of fashion. When gentlemen scoffed, Queen Victoria was "not amused."

Within the narrowing field of their cultivated ignorance, the young gentlemen prepared themselves vigorously for Parliamentary and administrative careers, and they developed an enthusiasm for open-air sport and that primitive form of bath called the Englishman's tub, which was quite outside the ideology of their Tudor and Stuart ancestors. Many of them still shoot with distinction; others devote much time and attention to fly-fishing; others again cultivate gardens and watch birds. They have developed a peculiar literature of their own; memoirs, biographies and autobiographies, collections of letters and speeches, which establish their social values and supply them with patterns for the careers they follow. This constitutes the bulk of their reading. So equipped, the British oligarchy, at the head of a vast and scattered medley of dominions, crown colonies, mandated territories, India, faces the vast occasions of our time.

It is questionable whether it faces them with any ideas about their future at all. Or its own future or any future. Like the Catholic Church, its main purpose seems to be to hold on, aimless except for self-preservation. It means to go on with the sort of life its fathers have left it, forever if possible, and that apparently is all it means. Crown, Church, lords and gentry will just stick at what they are where they are, until something shatters and replaces them. And they will do this not out of any essential wickedness but because in fact they know of nothing better to do.

The English-speaking world produces an abundance of

## THE BRITISH OLIGARCHY

thought and new ideas, and it has a reading public sufficiently large to secure the translation of any really original book written in any language under the sun. But that reading public is widely dispersed and the major part of it is probably outside the boundaries of the Empire. The British ruling class is shy of ideas and imaginative creation, it dreads and hates what it calls highbrow conversation, and it can have very little time to explore beyond its distinctive literature of personalities. A number of concepts and understandings, a vast multitude of facts, that are known and clear to all well-informed peope, seem never to have entered the British ruling-class mind or to have entered it only in a crippled or belittled state.

Here again, just as in our examination of the mutual unawareness of Catholicism and skepticism, we may fall into the error of imagining that what is known to us must necessarily be known to other people. But in reality these people who rule the British Empire do not willfully ignore a great number of things, they are simply ignorant of them or ignorant about them—which is quite a different matter. Ever since the first French Revolution, for example, the mind of the British ruling class has remained barred against any understanding of revolutionary democratic ideas. The French Revolution frightened them and they pulled down the blinds upon it. They chose to think that liberty means nobody doing any work, that equality means bringing the under-housemaid up into the drawing-room and sitting her down to play the grand piano, to her and the general embarrassment, and that fraternity means embracing extremely unwashed—untubbed—people. Socialism again they regard as a dividing-up of all the property in the world into exactly equal shares for everyone. ("Inequality would come again tomorrow.")

Since the advent of a real social democracy would certainly mean very profound readjustments in life for them, these quick shorthand interpretations so to speak, are far more satisfying and sufficient than a sustained argument. They insist upon thinking like that, and if their sons and daughters get other ideas they discourage them and "laugh them out of it" if they can. Everything indeed outside that little anecdotal world of theirs with its importances and routines, that world they would like to go on forever, they know as little about as possible; and since they have never looked at such projects and interpretations directly and intelligently, they cease to be projects and interpretations and are apprehended vaguely as prowling monsters, threats and perils—the Red Peril, the Yellow Peril, the Black Peril—outside rational existence altogether.

I have had plentiful opportunity of sounding the minds of socially well-placed people, and in common with all the world I have watched the political conduct of the Empire during the past few searching years. Manifestly the mentality now ruling is one in which "Bolshies" are the enemies of God and man, men who go east are "pukka sahibs," royalties, beloved mascots whose very pet dogs are adorable, and workers honest drudges so long as they are not "spoilt," with only one weakness, susceptibility to foreign agitators. Americans it is understood are snobs in grain, but rich, and they should be kindly entreated. They will just simply fall down before the dear king and queen, whenever they get a chance. And also remember, "they cannot afford to see the British Empire overthrown."

If the men get a little away from that sort of thing, the chatter of their women brings them back to it. Their women interfere a lot; the Colonel's lady is the typical figure of feminine influence throughout the social scale. In the army, in the Church, in politics, her good word raises up or casts down. All this is recognized openly in novels, in plays and social intercourse, but when it comes to political discussion and *Times* leading articles, then reality has to be wrapped up in a lofty pretentiousness. . . .

This is undignified writing. This is in the worst possible taste. Yet I cannot explain the twists and turns of Mr. Neville Chamberlain unless I use the terms I do. How can I adorn him with splendid prose? I cannot see him as anything but essentially ignorant, narrow-minded, subconsciously timid, cunning and inordinately vain. He and his father, Joseph, before him appear to me as the appointed scavengers of the fading Imperial dream. Joseph Chamberlain, with his mean yet extravagant idea of monopolizing the vast resources under the flag by means of an Empire *Zollverein,* aroused that convergent hostility of the Have-Not States, to which his son, with a sort of poetic justice, now makes his propitiatory surrenders.

I do not think Mr. Chamberlain wants to "save the Empire." The Empire came and the Empire may have to go. He adheres to something less transitory. His more immediate purpose, unless all his acts belie him, is to save the oligarchy and its way of life from its predestined end. He cannot understand that that way of life is over forever.

His family have been at such pains to achieve it, have been so eager, so clumsily eager, to serve it. Still he and his kind dream of friendly hospitable châteaux in a restored Holy Roman Empire or under a Spanish monarchy, and of a France, an Italy, a Greece made safe for the gentry again by the crushing out of all subversive forces. That I am convinced gives the ultimate range of the political vision of Mr. Chamberlain and his class.

When New York made an Exhibition to stimulate imaginations about *The World of Tomorrow,* the British pavilion stressed the sentimental past, exhibited Magna Carta, crown jewels, pedigrees and an old English village. There was a genealogical diagram to demonstrate that George Washington was "one of us." There was not the faintest anticipation of that great fusion of English-speaking thought and activity throughout the world, of which all modern-minded men are dreaming. World Federation? Instead there was the most definite reminder that the British Crown and Church stood gently but inexorably in the way of anything of the sort.

In the days before "Tariff Reform," it was possible for young Englishmen to dream of the Empire as a great propaganda and medium for liberal and broadening democratic methods, free migration, free trade and open speech, steadily weaving all the world together. It was a dream that captured many an alien imagination, as for example, Joseph Conrad's, but now it is an altogether abandoned dream. The idea of the Empire as a step towards world unification has lost all plausibility, and while the Chamberlain school of statecraft engages in its propitiatory dispersal, the creative

## THE BRITISH OLIGARCHY 165

imagination turns to the still living possibilities of one common culture of the English-speaking peoples.

An increasing number of British people look now to the present President of the United States for some sort of world leadership. He is a good, liberal-minded fellow anyhow, but in a sort of despair of anything better they do their best to exaggerate him. Britain herself produces no one to speak whatever liberal thoughts she has to the world. She has nobody of that quality, and even were there such a man it is difficult to imagine how under existing conditions he could emerge to popular attention. Without an objective, dumb, the Empire is becoming an anachronism, an Empire of passive and inadequate resistance. Its progressive disarticulation seems inevitable, and if after all the dream of a federal reassembling of the English-speaking and English-reading communities struggles towards realization, it will owe very little to the Imperial tradition and organization. North America, with its looser, freer and more abundant mental activities, is far more likely to become the backbone of such a reconstruction, and to carry it out on a democratic rather than oligarchic ideology. Monarchy, Church, influential families, experienced administrators and old Parliamentary hands, would merely clog and encumber the development of the social machinery necessary for a modernized world state.

So far from exercising any further leadership in world affairs, Great Britain is much more likely to withdraw into itself. With a dwindling population, an inadequately progressive educational system falling more and more behind the headlong needs of our time, and a shriveled prestige, the island may become unimportant enough to stand out altogether from the effort to effect a world synthesis. It may remain a crowned oligarchy yet for many years, fatuously content with itself and still as unaware as it is today of its continual decadence. Today in the Eastern world one can find a dozen anticipatory parallels, the self-satisfied and self-contained vestiges of what were once proud and important ruling powers.

Possibly this residual Old England, in addition to its hunting and shooting and fishing and race meetings and so forth, will carry on, will be almost forced to carry on, a small but bickering warfare with the equally decadent dictatorship of Catholic Ireland. In that manner, if the world fails to reconstruct itself, the British Islands seem likely to pass into the gathering darkness of the future. And if after all, mankind as a whole does meet the challenge of facts and the scientifically organized world state emerges, it will be into enlightenment rather than darkness that these island residues will dissolve. Macaulay's New Zealander may arrive after all, and when, according to the prophecy, he has visited the ruins of St. Paul's, he will be shown over the Houses of Parliament ("curious and rewarding," as Baedeker would put it) and do his puzzled best to imagine what that strange narrow life was like, assisted by extracts from Hansard, carefully preserved gramophone records of important speeches, enlarged photographs of Mr. Gladstone, movie glimpses of Mr. Neville Chamberlain in a state of indignation, and the still surviving political novels of Mrs. Humphry Ward.

## 18

### SHINTOISM

AND NOW WE MAY consider another great mental system ruling the minds and behavior of millions of men and women, which has recently become a leading factor in world destiny. This is Shinto, the official and compulsory religion of the Japanese. Formally, other religions are still tolerated, the Roman Catholic for example, but only on condition of ceremonial and practical acquiescence in the main doctrine of the creed, the recognition of the supreme divinity of the Mikado. Mr. A. Morgan Young has recently published an admirable summary of this culture,[1] and to this mainly I am indebted for the material of this section. He in turn gives his sources for whatever statements he makes, so that the interested reader can easily verify and expand what is given here.

The basis of Shinto is the Kojiki, a compilation of the eighth century A.D. It is readable in its entirety only by scholars, its language being far more remote from the Japanese of today than eighth-century Anglo-Saxon would be from current English. For various reasons only portions of it have been modernized for general use. It begins with a sort of storm of Gods neither made nor begotten but

[1] *The Rise of a Pagan State* (1939).

passing away. From this tumult emerge two highly sexual figures, Izanagi and Izanami, who might be described in Hollywood language as male and female "sex appeal." They respond to each other with tremendous vigor, begetting gods and islands and at last a Fire God who burns up his mother Izanami. But by this time Izanagi is so set on procreation that everything about him procreates; he throws off his clothes and they become sea gods and land gods. Finally he produces the Sun Goddess from his left eye, the Moon God from his right eye and the headlong Susa-no-o by blowing his nose. After which he seems to have retired and the Sun Goddess and Susa-no-o occupy the stage.

After various remarkable adventures, no doubt of the greatest spiritual significance and full of lessons for the true believer, Susa-no-o meets a formidable damsel-devouring dragon with eight heads and other alarming accessories, makes the beast drunk with saki, and then kills it and cuts it up. But one of the tails resists and breaks his sword, because in it there is hidden a better sword. This he extracts and presents to his sister the Sun Goddess. It lies today, thickly swathed in brocade, in the Family Shrine of the Imperial House in Tokio. It is one of the Three Sacred Treasures, the sword, the mirror and the jewel, which the Sun Goddess transmitted to her heirs, the divine Emperors, the living Gods of Japan.

To the Western mind accustomed to a widely different system of myths and absurdities, this reads like monstrous nonsense. But it is wiser not to say that in Japan. For example, Mr. Morgan Young tells of what befell Dr. Inoue Tetsujiro, a loyal but liberal-minded Shintoist who ventured to doubt the authenticity of the Three Sacred Treasures. He

## SHINTOISM

was denounced, his publisher was penalized, and he was expelled from the Imperial University. Later on, while attending the memorial service of a friend, he was set upon by a gang of pious ruffians and beaten so that one eye was destroyed. So much for a man who had attempted to spiritualize and rationalize the Japanese faith. No one was punished for the outrage upon him, which indeed is only one sample among many of the spirit of renascent Shintoism. It is quite good form to jump at a man who uses a phrase or makes a gesture that seems lacking in piety, and stab him. It is like those fierce old colonels in England who assault people for not standing stiff to "God Save the King."

Mr. Morgan Young makes some interesting suggestions about the temperamental make-up of the Japanese. There are important Mongolian strains in them, but he quotes Putnam Weale *(The Truth about China and Japan)* to support the thesis that the virile and dominating factor is Malay. Their clothing beneath the kimono, the construction of their houses, their lapses into moody murderousness are all Malay. He insists upon the constant recurrence of head hunting proclivities in their history. An unintelligent bloodthirstiness is in their nature and tradition. They have an inferiority complex with regard to Chinese and Western civilization, which takes the form of an extravagantly aggressive and assertive patriotism. I have followed my authorities in these generalizations. So far as official Japan is concerned they seem to be thoroughly justified. They account for the fact that the head of the state is not so much a leader as a mystically sacred symbol. The rulers of Japan today are Nazis without a Hitler, Fascists without a Mussolini. In the animal world an acephalous monster is sometimes tougher to tame or destroy than one with a head.

From the deliberate isolation of Japan in the seventeenth century—when all the bickering Christian sects and in particular Xavier's Jesuits were expelled, and the entry of foreigners and foreign travel prohibited absolutely—until the barrier was broken down by Commodore Perry in 1853, there was an age of internecine feuds and exciting strife of every sort. Vendettas were honored. The play of the *Forty-Seven Ronin,* the most popular of Japanese plays, is the heroic consummation of a vendetta, ending, after the decapitation of the initiator of the feud, with the hara-kiri of these forty-seven heroes. Japan was indeed a romantic head-hunting preserve for the tough. And among the tough everywhere loyalty to the gang is the supreme virtue, loyalty to the gang and no mercy for the flats, the serfs, the common cattle, outside the gang.

This is as true of the "wise guys" of Soho as it is of the gangsters of San Francisco. Wherever there are young men without proper employment the tough guy reappears. The ultimate sin is "squealing"; the crowning heroism is silence under the severest questioning; the master triumph is brilliant outrage. These gallant fellows in Japan would rape or try their swords on peasants without compunction. In such an atmosphere of swagger and loyalty lived the Daimios, the feudal noblemen, and their henchmen the Samurai, until the barriers were forced and the outer world broke in.

About the beginning of this century, the code of honor of these bickering toughs, the noble warrior's way of life, was idealized by a certain Dr. Nitobe, who wrote a book in English called *Bushido,* "through which the word was for many years far better known abroad than in Japan." He incorporated all the finest pretensions of European chivalry. His Samurai became the disciplined and fearless knights-errant of the world. It took in a lot of people—including myself. In *A Modern Utopia* (1905), the world was taken care of by an order of "Samurai." They assumed the role of the Syphograuntes in the original *Utopia,* and in that they anticipated the Communist Party commissars very strikingly. Since 1900 we have had, *inter alia,* the Nazis, the Fascists, the Phalangists. I was thinking with my generation.

In a lecture at the Sorbonne, in 1927, *Democracy under Revision,* I returned to that idea of a disciplined liberal "party." It arises naturally and inevitably out of the problem of contemporary indefiniteness and the relative ineffectiveness of intelligent people.

Perry's guns in 1853 aroused that ringed-in Japan of blood feuds, hara-kiri and heroic decapitations to the existence of a dangerous and aggressive outer world. The Japanese nobles and their Samurai, given over altogether to pride, realized their enormous practical inferiority. While they had been enjoying life after their fashion, the outer world had stolen a march on them. It was plain they had to modernize or succumb—like India, like Java. They had to learn the tricks of these foreigners and learn them quickly, their machinery, their weapons and generally how they did it. At first it seemed that Christianity might be part of the coveted advantages, and Japan thought seriously of making Christianity a state religion. After much recalcitrance and rebellion, the Shinto religion was revived and the country was unified under the divinity of the Mikado.

Happily for the renascent Japanese, the British Empire

suffers from practically incurable Russophobia. It is a constitutional disease of the British ruling class. Every assistance was given, material and mental, to the new forces of consolidation, and in the Russo-Japanese War (1904-1905) an Eastern Asiatic power shattered the prestige of Europe on land and sea alike. The Great War completed the job. After that there were no more inquiries for an adaptation of Christianity to the headship of a divine monarch—a slight improvement upon the Royal Headship of the Established Church of England. Instead of Christianity, Shinto, a genuine home product, came into its own.

And gradually, in association with the concentration of power in the warrior class, it has consolidated itself and all its absurdities as the sole religion of Japan, driving every alternative faith and conception underground. For the better part of the period of modernization since 1868, there has been a steady influx of Western science, Western ideas, Western radicalism into Japan. There were endless circles in which "advanced" ideas were discussed freely. With an astonishing swiftness that liberal Japan has disappeared. A few murders, a clean-up of schools and colleges, and the thing has been done. In the place of an intelligent people we face a national monomaniac. This, from our present point of view, is the most important aspect of the whole business.

With an apparent singleness of purpose Japan has flung itself into the attempted conquest of China and the most reckless defiance of the chief naval powers of the world. Here, as in the case of Nazi Germany, we are left asking, "Where have all these reasonable mitigating people gone?"

## SHINTOISM

"Where"—and this is perhaps even more to the point—"has the rational element gone in those who have succumbed?" So many who once talked liberalism, seem now to be wholehearted belligerent patriots.

Our essential theme in this book is the possibility of changing the mental superstructure, the knowledge, idea and habit system of mankind. In that we hope. The tremendous rapidity of this last Japanese change-over is almost incredible. Is it an irreversible process? And if so, what will it go on to next? Can it stand military defeat in China?

Many things seem possible in this catastrophic world of today, but one of the higher probabilities of the present world situation seems to be the failure of the Japanese attack on her greater neighbor. China has astonished the world by her tenacity, by the steady unification of her resistance, by the emergence of a sort of pervading militant wisdom. The Japanese have been stupendously energetic and stupendously unoriginal. There has been much detailed cunning in their operations but no essential wisdom. Desperadoes may murder many people but they cannot divide and rule a hostile country. What will happen in their heads as they realize defeat with nothing but that childish Shintoism of theirs and a tradition and cant of swaggering victory to sustain them?

Will it be wrath and social revenge? Many of these young warriors who landed in China full of the toughest dreams of heroism, victory, rape and authority, must now be in a state of profound disillusionment. They will have a sense of having been fooled. And in China—unless I underestimate the quality of Chinese and Communist propaganda—they will have met not only hardship but ideas. Sooner or later they must go back to a country where the endurance of the peasantry and the people has been tried to the breaking point.

Here are the same factors that existed in Russia in 1918, the factors for a crude and violent social revolt. There is no greater threat to a government than the return of a defeated army. It will go ill in such an event with nobles and dignitaries and priests, and it is quite among the possibilities of the next few years that the last divine heir of the Sun Goddess, shorn of all divinity, may share a parallel fate to that of the last Little Father of Russia. Then, starting from an even lower level than Russia in 1918, Japan will have to reconstruct its social and economic life.

That may be one possibility, but history never repeats itself exactly, and revolutionary methods have changed very greatly in the last twenty years. As one turns these matters over in the mind, China looms not merely as a military but as a mental reality of the first importance. What systems of thought are operative there, what new systems of thought are worming their way into the brains—and many authorities declare that they are rather above the human average—of that immense multitude? That is a question of more importance in a forecast of the human outlook than any we have hitherto discussed.

# 19

## THE CHINESE OUTLOOK

THE PRIMARY IMPORTANCE OF China in the current interplay of human forces is due not only to the fact that it is the greatest mass of human beings with any sort of solidarity in the world, but also to its manifest educability. It is not only the largest but now it is probably the most plastic mass on earth. Hitherto we have been weighing the influence and destinies of set and blinkered cultures. But in China, tradition, cultural ideas, cultural methods are passing through a phase of extreme dissolution, the mind of every intelligent man is in a state of stimulated inquiry, and creative propositions, if they could be presented there, would surely have a freedom and effectiveness such as no other part of the world can display.

The immemorial basis of Chinese life is an industrious peasantry, the primary source of wealth, on whom the landlord, the loan manager, the merchant, the tax collector have lived in a state of inconsiderate refinement for a long period. When the pressure of taxation or population becomes intolerable, the peasant becomes a bandit and the tension is relieved. Bandits, says J. D. M. Pringle, are the Chinese equivalent of the "unemployed," they levy an unsystematic dole. There have never been any fixed impediments to peasants acquiring wealth or gentlefolk becoming poor, and so, though there has always been much poverty, it has produced little class antagonism. No race difference exists between rich and poor; there is no superimposed nobility, no chivalry with a strong military and hunting tradition. The absence of great natural barriers led to a precocious expansion of governments to a size that, almost from the outset, made a class of literate administrators more necessary and more important than soldiers.

The early need for writing in China arrested its development beyond a quasi-pictorial and clumsily elaborate stage. It was wanted too soon, before it could undergo simplification into a syllabic or alphabetical system. This also contributed to the distinctive quality of China, to the Chinese—if we may coin a word—*para-democracy*. The extreme difficulty of the written language did indeed put popular education out of the question and set a practical barrier between literate and illiterate more effective as between man and man than any Western class distinction, but at the same time the very difficulty of scholarship obliged the mandarinate to draw continually upon the clever sons of poorish homes. These special conditions converged to give China its distinctive social and political structure, a structure so difficult to alter without complete destruction, that so far neither invasion nor civil commotion has ever changed it in any essential particular. When for example the Manchus conquered the land, they merely founded a new dynasty and imposed the now vanished pigtail—rather by way of assimilation than subjugation. So far. But now this refractory system has to face something more powerful than Hun or Manchu or

Japanese; it has to face the change of scale, the change of pace, that is shattering all other human societies.

The religious basis of the Chinese system is equally in contrast with the God-centered beliefs of the West. Confucianism, Taoism and Buddhism are all alike atheisms. There is no one God standing in any personal relationship to man. Confucianism is concerned entirely with the present life, it discourages speculation and inculcates an excessive ancestor worship and respect for the state. It insists upon public service and dignified self-control, not to please a god but simply because that is the right way of living. Taoism is in contrast a religion of abandonment to nature. Politically it is anarchistic and around it cluster a great accumulation of superstitions, spiritualisms, spookisms and quasi-magic beliefs, incantations and astrology. Every folly of the wonder-lovers of today has been anticipated by Taoism. Buddhism teaches a transmigration of souls, souls that may be entirely unaware that the good and evil they experience is due to their behavior in a previous embodiment.

Essentially these religions are behavior systems—or misbehavior systems. Taoism is frankly anti-social, an imaginative dissipation of the mind and will, and Buddhism is at least a withdrawal from life. They are both what it is now fashionable to call escape systems. Their teaching finds its Western equivalent in the "detachment" of Mr. Aldous Huxley. Both foster religious orders and inflict a great multitude of monks and nuns upon the community, and neither has anything of importance to contribute to that intelligent reconditioning of the human mind which the present world situation demands. Politically and educationally, the yellow (or gray) clad Buddhist monk with his begging bowl and his pimping possibilities is a social nuisance; the convent passes by insensible degrees into a common brothel.[1] But Confucianism is almost pedantically upright. It is the religion of a respectable totalitarianism. Whatever political backbone is found among the older generation of Chinese is in the tradition of Mencius, the disciple and exponent of the master.

In the crucial period of the nineteenth century, China was more self-satisfied with itself than Japan, and altogether indisposed for fundamental change. It had no such sudden shock as Commander Perry gave the Japanese, and it had no consciously ruling caste to react effectively to a warning. It knew the European better than the isolated Japanese, and it had long since formed a poor opinion of the physical and moral bustle and inelegance of Western living. It found the Westerners ugly, truculent and requiring cautious management; but although they had a variety of curious mechanical advantages it deemed them despicable. Since it took on an appearance of Westernization, China held out against modernization for half a century after the Japanese awakening. It endured much. We cannot even sketch that story here from the British Opium War onward. China's first reaction to these aggressions was violent xenophobia. This culminated in the Boxer outbreak (1900) and the punitive looting of the Summer Palace at Peking by the allied European powers. Still China would not pull itself together to fight. Outlying parts of its Empire fell away; ports and provinces were seized; this did not affect the routine in the regions still intact. Even under direct foreign rule much of the old life still carried on. The ancient order seemed as incurably contented with itself as the British.

[1] See Lin Yutang's *My Country and my People* (1936).

## THE CHINESE OUTLOOK

Here is how that keen and witty writer Mr. Lin Yutang characterized the Chinese way of living—so recently as 1936. ". . . Face, Fate and Favor. These three sisters have always ruled China, and are ruling China still. The only revolution that is real and that is worth while is a revolution against this female triad. The trouble is that these three women are so human and so charming. They corrupt our priests, flatter our rulers, protect the powerful, seduce the rich, hypnotize the poor, bribe the ambitious and demoralize the revolutionary camp. They paralyze justice, render ineffective all paper constitutions, scorn at democracy, contemn the law, make a laughing stock of the people's rights, violate all traffic rules and club regulations, and ride roughshod over the people's home gardens. If they were tyrants, or if they were ugly, like the Furies, their reign might not endure so long; but their voices are soft, their ways are gentle, their feet tread noiselessly over the law courts, and their fingers move silently, expertly, putting the machinery of justice out of order while they caress the judge's cheeks. Yes, it is immeasurably comfortable to worship in the shrine of these pagan women."

So Mr. Lin Yutang in 1936, and in 1936 he still despaired of any purposeful consolidation of his country for many years to come. But in three years Japanese military savagery has brought about a desperate unification beyond any foresight.

Mr. Lin Yutang is by nature and disposition a Taoist of the finer sort. He betrays at times a certain patriotic uneasiness and impatience, but these are lapses from his usual artistic self. For the most part he sustains a genteel detachment from the revolution of 1911 which ended the Manchu regime and the pigtail forever. He deplores the novel energy of Sun Yat Sen who "kept up his reading." He notes that Chiang Kai Shek and his financial ally T. V. Soong work "like horses." His heart turns back to "Merry old China" in all the infinite strength of laziness. "The racial tradition," he concludes, "is so strong that its fundamental pattern of life will always remain."

Nothing in the world is so perennial as that. The history of China since the fall of the Manchus displays altogether new forces at work. It is not the old, old story. However reluctantly, she now faces towards Cosmopolis. The republic was the creation of Chinese students who had been educated abroad or by foreign missions, and mostly they had been trained in America. Never before had there been a Chinese revolution fostered in exile. But this last one, like the kindred Russian one, was made by expatriates. Its revolutionary technique followed Western patterns. The Chinese Republicans borrowed ideas from the Communist Party, and the organization of the Kuomintang provided a nexus for the restless and intelligent throughout the Empire. Numerically the Kuomintang, like the Communist Party in Russia in 1917, was a relatively small organization, but it was the only thing that had continuity and a definite will of its own in an otherwise planless chaos.

This is not the place to review the stormy confusion of Chinese affairs since the establishment of the Republic;[1] the experimental policies of Sun Yat Sen and the significance of his will, the treason of Yuan Shih Kai and his transitory usurpation of the Imperial throne, the clumsy attempts of the Russian Borodin to introduce an uncon-

---

[1] A compact summary is to be found in *China Struggles for Unity*, by J. D. M. Pringle and Marthe Rajchman.

genial class war and to revive xenophobia in the form of anti-British Imperialism as a fundamental motive. He failed, and returned to obscurity in Russia, but the Party, under Chou En-lai, organized a successful peasant communist state in Kiangsi—I say peasant communist because there was no attempt at collective farming—and a very efficient Red Army. Driven out of Kiangsi, this Red Army retreated fighting for six thousand miles in one of the greatest retreats in history, and stood at last with its back to Soviet Russia in Shensi and the northwest. The intricate struggles between the Nanking government, the private armies of various warlords and the Red Army, need not concern us, nor the romantic and mysterious cessation of the war against the "Reds." The fact became apparent to the Japanese that slowly and steadily China was being unified under one government. There was no time to lose. Like a fiery new birth came the tragic consolidation of the Chinese national spirit in the face of intolerable Japanese outrages. Today under the military and administrative ability of the energetic Chiang Kai Shek we have a China more united and purposeful than it has ever been before, and apart from its resolve for complete national emancipation, more incalculable than any other human aggregation.

So faded and nerveless are the old conceptions of life, so Taoist, that the entire collective mentality of China is now in effect a *tabula rasa* upon which it is possible to write almost any constructive idea. And what is written will be evidently determined very largely by movements in the general world mind outside the boundaries of China. The native contribution is in the nature not of initiatives but adaptive qualifications. Lin Yutang, in one of those involuntary lapses of his from "detachment" into patriotic distress and irritation, notes that a dozen years after the death of Sun Yat Sen, who is by universal consent the father of the new China, no Chinese writer has yet displayed the energy and intellectual power needed to write a full and competent account of the Founder's life and teaching. It would certainly be an immense commercial success; it would be of the greatest political importance; and in that land of lassitude, evasion and passive resistance to change, nobody produces it.

It would seem as though a Chinese mind must needs go abroad and lead a foreign life, before it can even begin to see China. And when it sees China it still depends upon a push from the exterior, for action.

The most vital new thing so far that has been written upon this blank Chinese intelligence is a sort of communism. In a later section we must examine communism as a world force, but here it is to be observed that just as Chinese democracy is not the same thing as Western democracy but a *para-democracy,* so Chinese communism is not by any means the Russian article, but a *para-communism.* It has rejected Borodin's crude ideas of liquidating the "rich," the class war and collectivized farming. It is essentially a peasant communism, a revolt against rent, taxes, debt, forestalling, speculative marketing and all the handicaps that enslave the little man. Its leaders are often the fanatical enthusiastic sons of wealthy men, sons who have read Marx and Lenin, but the responding rank and file are the commonalty. It educates earnestly and well, it carries on a propaganda by means of plays, concerts, meetings. It promotes a modernized script. It is making its people into newspaper readers. It is in fact producing a new sort of Chinese common man, with a genuine workers' and soldiers' solidarity. Everywhere the peasants, even those who do not belong to the Party formally, believe in it. Its "Red" Army is as sturdy as any China has ever seen, with partisan tactics peculiarly adapted to the country.

A second set of ideas which is being scrawled across the Chinese *tabula rasa* is the New Life movement. This was deliberately created by Chiang Kai Shek as a rival and substitute for communism. Chiang Kai Shek is at present the central figure on the Chinese stage; he has been fairly explicit about his ideas and motives, and there is considerable artlessness in what he says. He has an interestingly responsive and representative mind. He speaks with profound reverence of the influence of his mother in forming his character. She remained an earnest Buddhist to the end. She watched over his tender years. She trained him for an energetic life of public service and self-subordination. He took his early political leadership from Sun Yat Sen and the Kuomintang. Sun Yat Sen was a Methodist with a passionate desire to free his country from "Western Imperialism." This brought him at last into close association with the anti-Imperialist Borodin. It was Borodin's aggressiveness and the killing of rich people and foreigners that estranged Chiang Kai Shek from Sun Yat Sen.

Chiang Kai Shek became for a period militantly anti-Communist. His marriage with Miss Mayling Soong, a member of one of the richest families in China, may have had its subconscious influence upon him. His close association with the Soong family, and particularly with T. V. Soong, has relieved him of many temptations that have overcome other leaders less financially secure. Madame Chiang

Kai Shek is a woman of manifest beauty and force of character, and for some time she seems to have done the religious thinking for her husband. He was baptized as a Christian in 1930. Their type of Christianity is a simple evangelical bibliolatry, inclining to fundamentalism rather than to either modernism or Catholicism; it is fundamentalism with a dash of Buchmanism. Every day the Generalissimo reads his Bible and prays for guidance. He prays regularly and abundantly and says grace before he eats. In moments of doubt the sacred book is opened and consulted for an omen.

The New Life Movement is not however professedly Christian, though it speaks in the name of the Christian Sun Yat Sen. It is essentially a patriotic behavior system, attacking opium, polygamy and "immorality" generally, tobacco, alcohol, tea, coffee, meat. It is in violent reaction from the enervation of Taoist self-indulgence. It expresses the realization of the middle and upper classes that things are getting serious for them. Its ambition is to be stern and powerful, to promote a "clean" and strenuous life.

Chiang Kai Shek has been immensely impressed by Fascist and Nazi propaganda, he speaks in profound admiration of "the strength of present-day Italy and Germany," he swallows, as I did, the legend of Bushido (§ 18) and like Mr. Teeling (§ 13) he believes that the Nazi disciplines make for brotherhood, obedience and particularly for that "cleaner" life of sexual and imaginative suppression which leaves the mind free for militant authority. (Both he and Mr. Teeling would be all the wiser and better for a cleansing month in the latrines at Dachau.) But since the aim of the New Life is power even more than purity, it is flatly opposed to any infringement of the rights of private property. It was indeed primarily organized for that end, as a counterblast to communism, and by its emphatic denunciation of Communists and "traitors" and its rigid insistence upon the payments of debts, it makes a special appeal to foreign finance. Its Methodist virtues are a means to an end. The end is self-righteous power. No doubt the New Life stimulates the open campaign against opium, vice and insanitary living, and no doubt it releases a genuine streak of solemn masochism in the composition of the Generalissimo, but how far the natural Chinaman will give himself wholeheartedly to the New Life remains to be shown. The failure of Prohibition in America and the social demoralization caused by it, seem to have had no lesson for Chiang Kai Shek.

For my own part I believe in the complete honesty of Mr. and Mrs. Chiang Kai Shek, but it is plain that they have not the faintest conception of the demands that fate is making upon mankind. They sound indeed in all their published utterances, terribly limited and self-satisfied, and however much we may be pleased to see China led to victory against the Japanese, that is no reason why we should exaggerate the intelligence and vision of these two leaders, because they are instrumental in that hoped-for *débâcle*.

Such are the chief forces that are operating to produce the China of tomorrow—Chinese communism, or, to define it more clearly, *para-communism,* and this New Life which is plainly *para-fascism*. Neither is yet what one can call a commanding force. They combine against the common enemy, but they have no real convergence. The end of the war with Japan will release rather than conciliate their oppositions. China liberated will become more and more definitely a battleground of world ideologies. She will waver between Soviet Russia and fascism, between Christianity of the J. D. Rockefeller type on the one hand and a tentative socialism after the fashion of the New Deal, rather to the left of the New Deal, on the other. One may well doubt if she has any initiative of her own to give the world.

In most Chinamen there struggle a Confucian, a Taoist and a Bandit. To judge by the present state of things that completes the inventory. And yet there is an accumulation of artistic work, a record of invention and ingenuity to the credit of China, witnessing to something not covered by any of these three factors, to some constructive element that existing circumstances have failed to release, some higher intellectual development which may still be waiting there—for the proper evocation.

This raises what is from our present point of view a very important issue. Is there a real scientific modernism, a constructive originality, latent in that very respectable Chinese brain? Has it unexploited mental reserves? That is a question that might be extended far beyond the Chinese horizon. At present China is almost completely unaware of the ecological view of life. She has never heard about it. Science subsidizes no missions; it has failed even to organize its friends in defense of its own freedoms. Almost all this "new education" in China, that has been replacing the classics since the revolution, has been ear-marked for the service of some narrow dogmatism or other. Her brightest intelligences have had but a poor chance of any broader vision. So in China even more than in our Western world, political and social life is still a disastrous clashing-together of blinkered minds. What she thinks new is already old. She is no

## THE CHINESE OUTLOOK

more prepared to attack the gigantic problems of adjustment that close in upon her, in common with the rest of the world, than she was thirty years ago.

In these thirty years she has done great things. The greatest has been to discover and assert her national independence and solidarity. And still she has everything to do. It is either a prelude to renascence or failure, to have installed a Methodist Generalissimo in the place of the Son of Heaven, got rid of pigtails, given up smoking, drinking, swearing, necking and suchlike scandalous behavior, and driven the opium traffic underground. Things will not stay at that.

So China, because of its nascent state, because at present there is no deep-rooted system of ideas imposed upon her character and habits, presents, in the barest form, the universal human problem. What prospect is there of an effective drive towards a scientific understanding of history and present realities, and of a reconstruction upon the lines of that knowledge?

Here again we must repeat the refrain of this book.

There exist already scattered about the world, all the knowledge and imaginative material required to turn not merely these seething four hundred million people but the whole world into one incessantly progressive and happily interested world community. All that is needed is to assemble that scattered knowledge and these constructive ideas in an effective form. The world cannot go on, a hydra-headed confusion of sovereignties; it has to concentrate its direction in a World Brain. The organization of a few thousand workers and the expenditure of a few score million pounds could bring that indispensable organization into being. And I doubt if it will ever be done.

It would give this rudderless world, as it drifts towards the rocks, a chart-room, a compass, a bridge and steering-gear. . . .

It would change the face of human politics from the aimless stare of dementia to understanding purpose. . . .

To vary the image once more, in China, the greatest, most central and representative human accumulation in the world, the fields are manifestly "white unto harvest" for a comprehensive renewal of civilization, the whole land aches for it, and there are no reapers; there are only spreading fires, trampling beasts in the corn, and a few weaklings gathering a handful of ears.[1]

---

[1] A very convincing and readable picture of China in dissolution is to be found in Miss Nora Waln's *The House of Exile,* and there are also the various effective and well-informed novels of Mrs. Pearl Buck, *The Patriot* for example, and *The Good Earth.* Edgar Mowrer's *Mowrer in China* is a convenient little book, compact, full, and understanding.

20

## SUBJECT PEOPLES

ONLY VERY BRIEFLY AND, as it were, in parenthesis, is it possible to glance at the future of the black peoples massed in Africa and their kindred in America.

The argument of this book is framed on such a scale that the lives and deaths of scores of millions appear as details of microscopic size in relation to the general ant-hill. Moreover, it has a perspective of its own. It looks from the directive centers of human thought, outwardly. Estimates of the population of tropical and southern Africa vary round and about one hundred and fifty million. Probably it is subject to considerable fluctuations. These millions live, hope, desire and suffer. But this great population is so remote from the central intellectual processes of mankind, it contributes so little to these processes, that it counts for far less than the sixteen million Jews, from whom, in spite of great handicaps, come men of science, original thinkers, mental workers of all sorts by the thousand. Later, but many decades later, the Negro mind may make a steadily increasing contribution to the World Brain. But at present it is held off by such a tangle of difficulties, obstructions and mind-traps as only the rarest and luckiest of natural geniuses may hope to overcome.

In Lord Hailey's *An African Survey* (1938) and in Julian

Huxley's *Africa View* (1931), the reader may learn something of that tangle. There, for example, he will find a discussion of the language problem. Is the young Negro of genius to begin his learning in some narrow dialect or in such a wider medium as Swahili, which still provides only a very limited literature for his study, or shall he be given as soon as possible the key to contemporary knowledge and thought, in English or some other European tongue? And where are the teachers and schools to be found for that? Even if he gets English, will it be good, fresh English? Will he encounter anything better than the faded methods, half a century stale, of a lower type of English school? Will it let him get to anything better than Bible Christianity, the history of England and a nice Christmas story or so about holly and robins? Where the Negro is apt to become a little ridiculous is in his exaggerated response to white religious teaching. He takes it in good faith and brings out its absurdities. That is not his fault. *Green Pastures* and Father Divine are products of white revivalist teaching; they are not native African creations. They smell of the camp meeting and not of the Heart of Darkness. We have no right to call a Negro a fool when it is our people who have made a fool of him. Julian Huxley insists very definitely on the desirability of biology and descriptive geography as the backbone of native African education and on the natural interest and aptitude of the African for such studies. There he would be on his own ground. But because the African is ready for the right education, it does not follow that the governments in authority over him are. These poor-white schoolmasters can teach him nothing of the sort, because they know none of it themselves.

## SUBJECT PEOPLES

There is a great conflict of testimony about the abilities of black Africa. His bitterest detractors are unable to deny the Negro an enviable sense of rhythm, natural good-humor and an instinct for civility, a sense of fun, brilliant mimicry, rich artistic aptitudes. And more than that. In the United States, in spite of the severest handicaps, black men have been able to struggle up to do distinguished scientific and literary work, and in South Africa it has been found necessary to protect skilled white labor from the competition of able colored people by discriminating against the apprenticing of natives to skilled trades and restricting "certificates of competency" in various mechanical employments to whites. Obviously you cannot put up barriers to protect yourself from the colored man and at the same time declare that he is incurably your inferior.

The outlook for tropical and sub-tropical Negro life in the coming years is dark and indefinite. An adequate education, that would make a large proportion of that population conscious world-citizens, seems improbable, and the utilization of that great reservoir of ignorant animal vitality as a source of conscript soldiers or conscript laborers is highly probable. It is one of the good marks in the checkered record of British Imperialism that in Nigeria it has stood out against the development of the plantation system and protected the autonomy of the native cultivator—with the most satisfactory consequences to everyone concerned. But against that one has to set the ideas of white-man-mastery associated with Cecil Rhodes and sustained today by General Smuts, which look to an entire and permanent economic, social and political discrimination between the lordly white and his natural serf, the native African. And this in the face of the

Zulu and Basuto, the most intelligent and successful of native African peoples. The ethnological fantasies of Nazi Germany find a substantial echo in the resolve of the two and a half million Afrikanders to sustain, from the Cape to Kenya, an axis of white masters (preferably of Dutch origin and speaking Afrikaans) with a special philosophy of great totalitarian possibility called holism, lording it over a subjugated but much more prolific, black population.

That racial antagonism makes the outlook of South Africa quite different from that of most of the other pseudo-British "democracies." Obviously it is not a democracy at all, and plainly it is heading towards a regime of race terrorism on lines parallel and sympathetic with the Nazi ideal. The Afrikander will do his best to be a terrific fellow to the last, and he will see to it that the black insurrection gathering under his heel, is sufficiently under-educated and sufficiently embittered to behave savagely when its day of opportunity comes. He will always be rather afraid, and his fears will brutalize his treatment of his helots until he is intolerable. Slowly but surely a racial self-consciousness, a collective resentment, is being forced upon the Negro, not only in South Africa but throughout the world, and South Africa seems the inevitable theater for its release.

But the fate of South Africa need not concern us now, beyond the plain probability that whether the Dominion follows the fate of Haiti or San Domingo or whether the sjambok holds its own, it is very unlikely to contribute anything of primary value to the reconstruction of human society upon a planetary scale.

And so, too, we cannot consider here the possible survival or disappearance of that little group of human beings, the

Australian blackfellows, with their undeniable artistry, their aptitude for mechanical work, and so subtle a sense of form that they invented the boomerang ages before the white man made his first experiments with the much simpler propeller. Nor can we bring in that great festoon of interesting and distinctive human societies which hangs across the subtropical seas from Singapore in the west throughout the Dutch East Indies and New Guinea to Guam in the east. Sixty million brown and yellow peoples they are, illiterate, unawakened, but for the most part excessively polite and subservient.

The problem of all these colored peoples is a vast one, but vast as it is, it is still secondary to greater decisions. If the mind of the world can be pulled together so as to give our species a collective rational guidance, this problem will fall into proportion and be solved deliberately and sanely. The colored man will understand and be understood, he will get his fair chance, so that he will come at last to look the white man in the eye, feeling as equal to him as a musician does to an engineer, with as complete an acceptance of difference and as complete a mutual respect. But if we cannot achieve that intellectual readjustment, then the prospect is fear and more fear, cruelty and more cruelty, trampling suppressions, wild insurrections, massacres and reprisals, atrocities and counter-atrocities, and the ultimate waste of every good possibility in these still largely unbroached reservoirs of human variety.

It is not in their own lands that the destiny of all these people will be determined. It is not on the "illimitable veldt" or in the tropical forest, not in mountain fastnesses or on stormy seas that their hope is to be found. Natural aptitude is not enough. The inherent intellectual quality of a cannibal savage or a coolie laborer, a starving share-cropper or an Abyssinian slave, may be as high or higher than that of a distinguished professor or a brilliant colonial administrator, but the latter is not simply his inherent self; he is that plus an education. The one is like a photographic plate that has been casually exposed to the light, it is an accidental blur; it means little or nothing. The other is a plate that has been exposed in a carefully focused camera. It means. It is related. The education and habits of behavior it imposes are the greater part of the civilized man. The better and fuller his education, the better the knowledge organization of his life, the higher he stands over the bare human being, and the more he and his kind control him and are responsible for human destiny. The only salvation of these threatened millions lies through the patient, incessant ordering of the collective human mind. A man working in a study at Harvard or a student sitting, as Marx and Lenin sat in their time, in the Reading Room of the British Museum, may be linking ideas and devising phrases that will open the way of escape for all these menaced and benighted peoples to equal participation in a reconstructed world.

And here is the place to apply the same line of reasoning to that great miscellany of peoples and cultures which is India. They seem destined to play only a secondary and supporting role in any unification of human affairs that is achieved, not by reason of any inherent inferiority, but because they are debarred by their complicated mental barriers and divisions from any collective understanding of modern constructive ideas. These hundreds of millions also I see as people struggling in a net. At present none of their cultural

## SUBJECT PEOPLES

movements displays an original line of its own that amounts even to a slight contribution to world reorganization. Vague aspirations to an obviously fictitious nationalism of an imitative parliamentary kind, sustained by non-co-operation, preferential trading and the fasts of Mr. Gandhi, point to anything but the coming city of mankind. Starving on the doorsteps of the ruler in the Gandhi fashion is a curiously unfair appeal to the ruler's decency. Directly it is used against anyone tough enough to say "Starve then, and be damned to you," it becomes ineffective.

There would be much to be said for an Indian nationalism based upon the idea of human brotherhood and the common future of mankind. If all these peoples can be fused, the whole world can be fused. But speaking generally Indian nationalism is no sort of synthesis; it is based on a common, understandable resentment at the British Imperial Government and on very little else. You cannot build a nation on a vanishing grievance. The old Raj is not going to last forever, and when it fades out the Hindu will still be wearing his caste marks and the Moslem slaughtering cattle at him in a derisive spirit.

A culture which said "We are ignorant and divided and condemned to a collective sterility by our ignorance, and we mean to reorganize our mental energy and stock our minds to play our proper part in human unity," would be a culture to respect. But even the Brahmo Sumaj, most liberal of Indian cultures, does not say that. It is universalist religiously, but it is not acutely educational. In India there are numerous rich men, great industrialists, wealthy maharajas and the like, but it has still to dawn upon any of them that a great, growing, liberating mass of knowledge exists in the world beyond the present reach of any Indian, and that there must be scores and hundreds of thousands of fine brains, which need only educational emancipation and opportunity, laboratories, colleges, publication facilities, discussion with the rest of the world, to add a continually increasing Indian contribution to the ever-learning, ever-growing World Brain. In India now there must be a score of potential unrealized Royal Societies, so to speak, running about in loin cloths and significant turbans and Gandhi caps and what not, running about at that lowly partisan level, and so running to waste.

The British ruling class has been unable to impose modern ideas upon India for the simple reason that it does not possess them itself. The indebtedness is the other way round. The British picked up the idea of caste from the Brahmins and gave very little in return. And other things they picked up. I do not know if anyone has ever made an estimate of the number of elderly gentlemen who return to Great Britain with gurus in tow, mysterious dodges for breathing down their spinal canals, Yoga and all that. They seem to be quite numerous. Man for man when it comes down to that sort of thing the Hindu is master.

What modernization may come into Indian thought and life is much more likely to arrive tediously and belatedly from the north as an adapted communist propaganda, a propaganda modified perhaps by contact with whatever modern Western science may have come in by, through and in spite of British influence from the south.

## 21

### COMMUNISM AND RUSSIA

It is difficult to say whether on the whole dogmatic communism is to be regarded as a disaster that has happened to the growing discovery of the rational world state or an unavoidable phase in that discovery. In the earlier half of the nineteenth century and especially in the years of recovery from that embolism called Napoleon, there was a great bandying about of creative and pseudo-creative ideas, humanisms, varieties of socialisms, hand-specimen Socialist experiments, New Lanarks, Oneidas, Brook Farms. In all of them there was a subconscious feeling that something was still wanting, the ideas were incomplete. Such a phase of the collective mind is very distressful to impatient intelligences. They feel that nothing is being achieved; they want to "fix something and get on with it." At this pace, they feel, we shall get nowhere.

So they get into the ditch.

Apt to the demands of such eager spirits came Marx. He was a man of vast intellectual ambitions, emulous of Darwin and Adam Smith. He seized upon that economic aspect of life which the political revolution had ignored, and he hung on to that. The "capitalist system," which was his misnomer for privately owned capitalism, had to be abolished and then social justice would ensue. He proclaimed the materialistic conception of history and the class war as the only practicable way to social justice.

Neither Adam Smith nor Darwin, with whom he was obviously disposed to put himself in competition, betrayed any sense of finality in his thought nor any ambition for leadership. They contributed and passed on, according to the new scientific morality. But Marx was of a more primitive and more immediately practical type of intelligence. He was for conclusive formulation, for dogma and an energetic revolutionary effort according to that dogma. He evoked a vigorous, rigid-spirited movement for the destruction of "capitalism" by an insurrectionary class war. He had no ideas, and he was probably incapable of producing ideas, about the peace that should succeed victory in the class war. It never entered his head that a powerful new organization of knowledge and will would be required to direct an emancipated world system. He was, to be plain about it, too lazy-minded. He invented a phantom, more insubstantial than the Holy Ghost, the proletariat. The ever-blessed proletariat would see to it all.

The curious may read about that proletariat, and what is and what is not the dictatorship of the proletariat, and when the Party is the dictatorship and when it is not, and how the peasant comes in, in Joseph Stalin's *Leninism*. It is the Athanasian Creed of socialism.

But these complications arose later, and at first the proletariat *sans phrase* sufficed. That the proletariat would solve everything with the hammer of Thor and the sickle of Rhea Cybele was an all too attractive doctrine for eager minds, and the communist movement, in perfect unison,

## COMMUNISM AND RUSSIA

contemned and despised the intricate and difficult business of foresight as "utopianism," and scientific criticism as a sinful want of faith. And so at last when czarism and private ownership of land and capital did collapse in Russia, and that great country was thrown into the hands of the communist leaders, they were totally unprepared with any conceptions of a better organization of affairs.

The released Russia of October 1917 found itself wildly experimental. It had to reorganize a great community fallen into chaos, and it had only scraps of suggestion of how to set about it. Upon Lenin fell the immense task of rationalizing Marxism and getting it to work.

In § 6 the question "What is democracy?" is asked and answered, and it is shown that the life of a human being can be full and free only if it is politically, economically and mentally liberated; that is to say when it is living in a state of political equality, socialism and universal adequate education. Without that much realization, liberty, equality and fraternity are mere words. Marx and his Communist Party never fully grasped the third, the educational condition. How to direct? how to keep direction?: these were questions they never answered. They filled in the gap in their doctrines with that sprawling, muscular divinity with the hammer and sickle, who is in truth hardly more real than those symbolic Hindu gods with countless arms and extra parts who puzzle the realistic Western mind. Believe in Him, said they.

In practice the Russian Communists were less elusive than their creed. If they fudged a pseudo-God, in order to get on with their revolution, they were still acutely responsive to modern democratic ideas. They set themselves with considerable energy and success to liquidate the illiteracy of the common people, but unfortunately they did not go on with the harder task of educating themselves. They did not realize the need for that. Instead they suppressed disturbing discussion. They are today blinkered and boxed-in to an ideology as definitely restricted, within its wider limits, as that of the orthodox Jews, the British oligarchy, the Roman Catholic hierarchy or the Chinese patriots we have discussed in preceding sections.

The Russian spectacle for the last twenty years has played an immense part in the thought and imagination of the young everywhere. When everything that can be said has been said against it, it still seems to be ahead of the rest of the world in its progress towards the practical realization of the complete democratic idea. Whether it will go on and keep that lead is quite another matter, but the improvement not merely in the material circumstances but in the spirit of the common people is beyond dispute. They were servile and now they are proud. They have a wholesome conceit that the world looks to them. That has been done at a price, yet nowhere else has anything been done to compare with it. America also has advanced in its ideas, as we shall note in the next section, but it started far ahead, five centuries ahead, of Russia.

But Russia may have achieved this much progress less by virtue of the Communist Party than in spite of it. The Communist Party did no doubt bring the spirit of revolutionary progress to Russia, but it was not in itself the spirit of revolutionary progress. It might well have been better prepared for the task, and it might have produced men of a finer caliber and greater magnanimity. The darkest shadow on the Russian outlook today is its failure to produce a constellation of first-rate men able to evoke its general intelligence and speak for it to the world. Like most countries today, Russia does not seem to be putting her best men foremost. She does not know how to find them and use them. She goes on being clumsy. Russia is faltering and losing its imaginative appeal. Her inability to deal with her internal difficulties without a series of trials and executions, so presented as to be extraordinarily repugnant to the Western mind, and the open and undignified bickering of Trotsky and Stalin, have done much to rob her of her once almost magical fascination for the undergraduate intelligence. That intelligence is now shocked and puzzled. It may easily stampede in some new direction, and the real greatness of the new Russia may be forgotten altogether in its superficial littleness.

But how intolerable these ardent young Communists of the last fifteen years have been! What a rawness they have imparted to social and political discussion, all the world over! How unrighteously is the reasonable man tempted to rejoice at this present deflation of noisy, juvenile leftism! It is rare for the normal human being to attain to an adult mental independence before thirty, and it is rare for it to refrain from the vehement expression of opinions after eighteen. Satan finds some mischief still for idle youth to do. Its natural instinct is to rebel against its parents and the parental generation, which has brought it into the world for no end it finds explicable, and, since it is still much too timid intellectually to act alone, its disposition is to go over, lock, stock and barrel, to the organization in flattest repudiation of the flaccid home atmosphere. The good pagan's daughter goes Catholic and the Catholic's son goes Communist. And there they stick. They have made their little act of assertion, but they must still have the comforting feeling of something not themselves, something built up authoritatively, to which they can cling. The boy who runs away from home likes to get on to a ship and give himself up to that. If not, he usually comes home again.

It is one of the primary difficulties of this creature *Homo sapiens* that it grows up, so far as bodily and willful energy goes, twenty years before its mind has ripened enough for it to think and act alone. The young want to do vigorous and effective things by eighteen, while their mental unripeness obliges them still to seek authority for the things they want to do. They cannot wait. They will respond to nearly anything that lets their energy loose, as a kitten will pursue a cork on a string. There we have the common clue to the storming young Nazi, the Irish patriot, the Spanish Anarchist Syndicalist, the bomb-throwing Zionist, the Shinto militarist, the gangster, the Ku Klux Klansman. They are all forms imposed upon and accepted by that youthful surplus which is the imperative problem of our species, which will overstrain and wreck every social system until its insurgent need to be used is anticipated and satisfied. It has been made clear how this mental exuberance has been allayed in the past by wars and migrations, and why it is that these natural reliefs are no longer sufficient for the magnified destructive forces of the new time.

In the last three years in Britain there have been three magnetic movements with an unaccountable attraction for unemployed vitality. Fascism, a fourth possibility, was happily made repellently ridiculous for our sons in the person of Sir Oswald Mosley, but the impressionable young men who did not succumb to the God-guided woosh of Buchmanism or the high-toned Anglo-Catholicism of T. S. Eliot, fell very readily to the worship of the heroic Hammer-and-Sickle-God. They joined the Party, surrendered themselves to tasks and disciplines and strategies. They felt they had the revolution and all Russia behind them. How they maddened their serious elders, those undergraduates holding on without thought or question to the Party and being as rude as they knew how to critical liberalism, for all the world like naughty children holding on to nurse's apron strings and putting out their tongues at the grown-up passers-by!

That particular adhesion seems to be drawing to an end after the political and intellectual waste of a generation of silly, gallant young lives. They exaggerated the perfection and finality of Soviet Russia. Some have died for that faith. Now the drift is all against the present regime, and instead of searching criticism we are likely to have partisan condemnation. Yet there is a strong case for the existing regime in Russia.

There, there has been and there is still a sustained, widespread and honest effort to build up a new social and economic order. It is only necessary to contrast the Russian drive with the relative ineffectiveness of the Kuomintang. In Russia "revolution" still means, for millions of minds, a new human beginning. In no other community is that idea of a new beginning so manifestly at work. It had had to work against bad social traditions and a widespread defensive subtlety and disingenuousness, with a people to whom punctuality and precision were strange ideas. Chekhov lived and died before the war, but his stories are saturated with the distress felt by a man with a modern scientific training, at the all too human indiscipline of the land he loved. The Bolsheviks, planless themselves, as we have seen, had to take over that world, shattered, impoverished, chaotic, invaded from every direction, and make a working system of it, some sort of new order, however rough and clumsy, or perish. And they have made a new order, rough and clumsy still perhaps in many aspects, but holding together, really holding together, and not nearly so rough and clumsy as it might have been.

I have visited Russia thrice, in 1914, in 1920 and in 1934, I have had long talks with Lenin and Stalin, I have some well-informed and variously orientated Russian friends, and I have read a library full of books about Russia, *pro* and *con*. Like most of the world, I was amazed at those strange public trials and the killing-off of, among others, a majority of the original revolutionaries. And I think that of all my witnesses, I have learnt most from an American mining engineer, Mr. J. D. Littlepage, who wrote a book called *In Search of Soviet Gold*.

There never was a writer so free from the taint of political prepossessions. He is no sort of *ist* or *crat* at all. But he likes mining to be done properly and shipshape, no fudging, no shirking, no waste, no stealing, no trickery. You have to come down heavily on that sort of thing. He thinks vigorously within *his* blinkers (excellent blinkers) of honesty and high efficiency. And he tells the story of how he was engaged to revive and reorganize the Siberian mines, copper and other minerals as well as gold. He tells pretty convincingly—and it is illuminating—how Stalin was moved to start this revival, and of all the difficulties and complications of the task. At the Littlepage touch the vast, sinister phantoms of Trotskyite conspiracies and organized capitalist sabotage vanish from the scene, the confessions of the accused join the confessions of sorcerers during the witch mania, and we see the human reality of incompetent men trying to cover up the mess they are making of things, of wrongfully-appointed men holding on to their jobs by trick and subterfuge, of hates and jealousies, of elaborate misrepresentations to save the face of groups involved in a common failure, of the manufacture of countervailing evidence, counter-accusations, resort to influence in high quarters. These are the ways of imperfect, inadequately watched men everywhere. The allied generals on the western front during the great war behaved similarly, though unhappily there was nobody to shoot them. And at the last come the confessions, to put a consistent face on the untellable tale of fudging and muddle-headness. Better persuade yourself you are a consistent conspirator than a self-protective fumbler, a snake rather than a worm.

Littlepage makes you understand not only the slackness of the country and the disappointing output, but also the perplexity at the head of things, the inability to get sound information and to discriminate between merit and speciousness. The head does not know whom to believe, grows suspicious and incalculable. The impulse of most of us when we cannot hit accurately is to hit hard. The shootings become understandable; take on the quality of necessity. After Littlepage you can re-read the reports of those trials and begin to understand them. The wonder of Russia is that nevertheless so much has been done.

I write with prejudice about communism, but it is not prejudice on its behalf. I have made it clear, I think, how intensely I detest Karl Marx and how greatly my mind has been irritated by the narrowly dogmatic communism of the young. Yet I am forced to a recognition of the real advance Russia has made since the revolution, not merely in material things. Will it go on? What for us is the significance of the new phase into which Russia is now passing?

The mass of the new Russia still seems in its crude way to be revolutionary, in the best, the creative sense of the word. The great raw organism is still moving forward. But there is manifestly something wrong about the head of it. A great number of disillusioned young men in the Western world are saying now that it is Stalin who is to blame and proclaiming themselves Trotskyites. But the matter goes deeper than that. It is not really a personal matter. The organization at the head of things must be radically wrong to be put out of gear by a mere personal feud. It must be so framed as to eliminate good types of mind and promote mediocrities. Lenin was a first-quality man, Litvinov is a much abler man than the run of diplomatists; apart from that the personalities directing Russian affairs vary from honest ordinary to intricately mean. It is preposterous to suppose that they are the pick of that Russian intelligence which has produced men like Mendeleev, Mechnikov, Pavlov, Pushkin, Maxim Gorky....

The headquarters organization upon the shoulders of the Russian giant is, to be plain about it, a head without a forehead; it has a brain that lacks anything more than a rudimentary cerebrum. Russia, with an area of over eight million square miles and a gross population of one hundred and sixty-six million people, is being run by a directorate as antique and rudimentary in its nature as some small pronunciamento South American Republic or the tyranny of an ancient Greek city state. It has no knowledge organization at all. It has no powers of reflection. It has only the Communist Party—which is dogmatic ignorance. It is a giant— I speak of social structure and not of persons—with the head of a newt.

That is the absurd situation of Russia. Only, unhappily, nobody seems to consider it absurd. The country is still living on the mental impetus of Lenin and the democratic socialism of the nineteenth century. When that impetus is spent it will have nothing to fall back upon but the preposterous pretensions of personal government.

It is this absence of a collective cerebrum that has made the present feud of the Stalinists and the Trotskyites possible. Trotsky I have never met, but he seems to have a considerable personal vanity; Stalin I liked when I talked to him; I did not think he had an overwhelming intelligence, but I thought he was honest and strong and human. I have been disillusioned about him mainly by those foolish films of personal propaganda he has allowed to be made, *Lenin in October,* for example. Therein Trotsky is elaborately belittled and Stalin made the all-wise hero of the story. He stands over Lenin. Modestly but firmly he indicates the strategic points in the map and tells him what to do. Apparently he is trying to distort the whole history of the revolution for his personal glorification.

Why do these two men behave in this way? Apparently they are posing for posterity. That was something Lenin never did. He was a man of the new order. Both Trotsky and Stalin are middle-aged and have very few years left now in which to do anything more for the world, and this is how they dissipate them. They are behaving as absurdly as Mussolini. Few human beings are adult before thirty-five and most remain puerile to the end. Do they not understand that even if they are remembered they are—in the busy world ahead—certain to be misjudged? Nobody will have time to read whole books about them. One or another thing awaits these legends they are cherishing. If the world fails to readjust itself now, they will pass, with everything else that is human, into oblivion; and if it does readjust itself to its new occasions, then so far as they are remembered at all, they will be taken in hand by a more adult and motherly Clio and spanked and put in their places.

I am amazed at these egotisms and astonished at the complete inability of the Communist rank and file, out of Russia at any rate, to avoid taking sides. Either they take sides or they wander away from the idea of creative revolution altogether, so completely are they dependent on the behavior of their Great Men. This is infantile. The man of the new world order, if ever it is to be attained, must learn to go right on without leaders, just as he must learn to go right on without God.

What is happening to the body of Russia, obscured by this scuffle? The scuffle has so narrowed-down to personalities that a great deal may be happening outside it. It may be that in this matter my wish is father to my thought, but at any rate I believe that a more or less complete restoration of intellectual liberty in Russia in the next few years is a quite possible thing. The Russian, who, like the Englishman or the American, has grown up in an atmosphere of less immediate militant stress, is not nearly so docile as the German. There is an ineradicable disposition to humor and

## COMMUNISM AND RUSSIA 209

laughter in these less controlled peoples. They are earlier adult. I cannot suppose that the Nazi regime would tolerate for a moment those popular stories by Michael Zoshchenko, which hold up the weaknesses and discomforts of the Soviet regime to the gayest ridicule. Laughter can dissolve prison bars; it can outflank prohibitions. Russian writers are beginning to take liberties.

The Russian mind is an insubordinate mind and an untidy one. This virtue and this vice may be two aspects of one quality. Russian thought lacks and needs the restraint of the more disciplined Western intelligence. It has that courage and irresponsibility which we associate with genius. A release of intellectual energy in Russia, corresponding with and responding to the appearance of a reorganization of knowledge and collective purpose and judgment in the West, would have a vastly stimulating effect upon the thought and will of the entire world. It would be an event of major importance in the mental reorganization of mankind. And in the brightness of this new beginning it would hardly be observed that the Communist Party, the Comintern, too narrow, too insincerely dogmatic and "too clever by half," had unobtrusively disappeared, as I suppose that sooner or later it must do.[1]

[1] See F. Borkenau's *The Communist International* (1938), a history which is also an analysis.

## 22

### AMERICAN MENTALITY

FINALLY, IN THIS STOCKTAKING of human forces, we come to the countries more directly affected by the American and French revolutions, at the end of the eighteenth century, the countries in which, beyond the shadow of the British oligarchy, radical and liberal and democratic ideas have had a maximum freedom of expression. Chief of these, and charged now, it would seem, with the main burthen of their common destiny, is that third great mass of human beings with any sort of solidarity, the United States of America, China, Russia, North America; these vast countries make more than a third and nearly a half of humanity; they occupy most of the north temperate zone, which is the zone of maximum human energy, and with the British Empire they constitute the greater part of mankind. They are all fermenting with change. And the most freespoken, active, perplexing and various of all these great vats of destiny is the United States.

The United States is of primary significance in world affairs for a number of reasons. In the first place its population is almost entirely literate, that is to say, it can read. How it reads and what it reads is another matter. There are no cheap books in America such as there are in Great Britain

## AMERICAN MENTALITY

and France; most books worth reading can be got in England for sixpence, while in America they cost from ten times as much upward; and outside a limited world even prosperous people hear very little of any but those best sellers which follow each other like epidemics across the continent. But the newspaper Sunday supplements and the public libraries largely compensate for these present imperfections of the book supply. So the American public as a whole, over the vast areas it covers, is simultaneously accessible, if need be, to new ideas, and that accessibility is greatly enhanced by the nation-wide distribution of the cinema and the radio. And next it has a tradition of free discussion. The American says what he thinks, and even when he doesn't think he is apt to say it. You can always contradict him, and there is no handicap to help any opinion to win.

Education is in the hands of the forty-eight state governments of the Union, and varies widely in its standards and organization from state to state; schools, colleges and universities are scattered abundantly over the land; they range from sheer imposture upward, and the best of them are as good as or better than anything else in the world. There are great endowments for education and for educational enterprises. There are probably more highly educated people in the United States than in any other single country whatever, and when it comes to what we may call the half-educated, people whose minds, already loosely furnished, could easily be quickened, there is no comparison. In one or two backward states, modern scientific teaching—of evolution, for example—is prohibited in the state schools, and discriminatory obstacles are put in the way of the education of colored people. These are exceptions to a general freedom. The intellectual possibilities of this vast country are unlikely to be seriously threatened by invasion, extreme war stresses or civil convulsions for some time. They are threatened just enough to stimulate them and prevent their becoming lethargic.

Like all the rest of the world, the Union has felt the impact of the new conditions of human life, the progressive abolition of distance, the immense increase of material power and the ensuing dislocations of economic and social order, but less confusedly and with more time and elbow-room for consideration than any other country. It has been able to look and see; it has been able to think more plainly about the change that has come upon us all. It has only realized in the last decade that it has an accumulating surplus of unemployed.

There is a vast elementariness about the past hundred and fifty years in America. It is as if social and political life in the United States was simplified and made plain for demonstration purposes to all the rest of the world. We have there in unqualified contrast the East and the West, the North and the South, White and Black; no petty nationalisms, no traditional hatreds, no language difficulties, no localized religions obscure the broad issues. The War of Independence left the country a democracy, democracy at its first stage, the state of political equality and individual liberty. The extension of the democratic idea to include socialism, educational equality and universally accessible information, which we have traced in § 6, scarcely affected America until the close of the nineteenth century. Throughout all that century she worked out the possibilities for good and evil of a hard individualistic democracy. The Civil War, though it arose out of a number of economic and political stresses, simplified out at last, to a logical completion of the equalitarian idea by the abolition of slavery and the enfranchisement of the liberated slaves.

Life throughout that period resolved itself into a scramble for wealth. The whole nation thought dollars, talked dollars. For several generations it was a distinctly exhilarating scramble. There were so much unexploited land, such reserves of natural wealth available, that it was possible to accumulate vast fortunes and still find fresh employment for everyone who chose to work. After the civil war came a great development and organization of industry. American invention, American enterprise, soon led the world in the expansion of big business and the mechanization of life. For a time it was not realized that this march of Triumphant Democracy [1] was essentially the rape of virgin resources that could never be replaced. Triumphant Democracy poured across the continent, destroying the forests and so changing the climate for the worse, ploughing up pasture that presently became sandy desert, exterminating animal species, using up coal, oil, mineral wealth as though there was no end to any of these things.

It was only as the "Wonderful Century" drew to its end, that the immensity and the menace of Waste dawned upon people's minds. Everyone was so keen to get dollars that many of them forgot to get children, but the supply of labor for all that vast ploughing-up, cutting-down and tearing-out was sustained by a tremendous immigration. In 1906 a million immigrants poured into America, mostly people who knew no English and had a far lower standard of life than the native worker. They were divided among themselves

[1] Andrew Carnegie, *Triumphant Democracy* (1886).

at first by their special ignorances; they supplied a far more manageable type of labor from the point of view of the exploiting employer.[1] The home-grown strain hoped to save money, get on, escape from employment, and so it was slow to develop any class solidarity until it realized that every door to hopeful competition was being closed upon it. Labor legislation in America therefore fell far behind that of Great Britain. Not only was the immediate real wealth of America being turned to dollars; a rapid deterioration of the common life was also going on. Very reluctantly would America admit that the great uprush was over. Theodore Roosevelt's campaign for Conservation was the first practical recognition in America that Americanism had gone too far.

This is not a history, but a survey of existing possibilities, and we will say nothing here of the events that exalted and depressed American life for the next third of a century, the war, the boom, the collapse, until we come to that nationwide realization of crisis and panic that brought Franklin Roosevelt in as the savior of a staggering social system.

Sometimes a work of art can do more to present reality than a whole library of reports and statistics, and that tremendous genius, John Steinbeck, in his *Grapes of Wrath* (1939), has given an unforgettable picture of the last stage in that process of material and moral destruction and disillusionment with which the story of sturdy individualism in America concludes. He gives it all, from the exhausted soil dribbling down to dust, to the broken pride, the hopeless revolt and the black despair of the human victims, without rhetoric, without argument, but with an irresistible effect of fundamental truth.

[1] See my *The Future in America* (1906); *Two Studies in Disappointment*.

## AMERICAN MENTALITY

The crisis discovered a great man in Franklin Roosevelt. As I have written elsewhere,[1] he is a "patrician" rather in the vein of Lord Grey and Arthur Balfour than a typical American politician. He is rich and his peculiar health makes him float rather above the level of everyday temptations. He has the boldness of imagination needed to meet the challenges of the time, but he has the great gentleman's disposition to look to subordinates for the detailed execution of his designs. None too soon he has carried America forward to the second stage of democratic realization. His New Deal involves such collective controls of the national business that it would be absurd to call it anything but socialism, were it not for a prejudice lingering on from the old individualist days against that word.

At the beginning there was much talk of the Brain Trust, which he had gathered about him to realize the vast change-over of American affairs he had in hand. I was tremendously excited by this Brain Trust idea, and I went off to America, as my *Experiment in Autobiography* relates, to have a good look at it. He had imagined that the universities could and would give him men of exhaustive knowledge and capacity in sufficient amount to create, on the spur of the moment, a civil service competent to meet the huge demands of this great transition he was so gallantly attempting. These Brain Trusters were what the universities produced for him. My wits were not quick enough to size them up at once. They seemed to be an extremely interesting and miscellaneous set of men, but I had a feeling from the outset that they were not going to justify the President's expectations. He

---

[1] *Experiment in Autobiography*, Chapter IX, § 9, and *World Brain*, The Fall in America, 1937.

was under an easy delusion about the American universities. He thought they were untapped reservoirs of wisdom. They are not. They were quite unable to give him the knowledge, understanding and responsive imaginations necessary to convert his magnificent gestures of social and economic reconstruction into a working reality.

I went, a traveling note of interrogation, from him to Stalin, because I realized that the same insufficiency of mental resources and support which was baffling the American President, the lack of any adequate mass and structure of administrative knowledge in the state, must also be crippling the socialist thrust in Russia. Was Russia meeting or attempting to meet that difficulty? In some way of its own? And in Russia I found Gorky in a dream of Russia's greatness, unfolding the plans of non-existent universities to my incredulous eyes, and nothing else but intolerant dogmatists and intriguing commissars.

Both Roosevelt and Stalin were attempting to produce a huge, modern, scientifically organized, socialist state, the one out of a warning crisis and the other out of a chaos, and the lack of a brain organization to give that state consciousness and coherence was a difference not in nature, but degree.

The brain organization of the United States is not up to its new job. It needs to be revised, expanded, turned round to face the future. I have compared the head structure of the Russian giant to the brain of a newt. To carry on the biological analogy, the knowledge and will structures of the United States seem to be somewhere about the level of a horse. It has a cerebrum all right; it remembers almost too well within a limited range, it shies at shadows, stampedes very readily, and has no particular zeal for learning

## AMERICAN MENTALITY

new things. Something very much better than that is demanded.

For the great, closely-organized, human community that socialism contemplates, a World Brain is essential. The third aspect of a complete democracy is a tremendous educational expansion, that not only opens the way to the White House to Everyman but gives him the necessary mental equipment, if he can use it, to get there. Such an educational organization has been latent in America for a century and a half. The fathers of the Republic were not unmindful of it. In every state, land was set aside to supply the endowment for a state university, and sometimes that turned out well, and sometimes it did not. In addition, there were older endowments of the British type, and fresh benefactions expanded these and added to their number. The whole community was concentrated upon that fascinating dollar hunt, but when one of the winners felt public-spirited and generous, it seemed a fine thing to him to get some more knowledge and education for the people. And being essentially a business man, he went and bought the stuff; he bought the best in the market; and it did not occur to him—and why should it?—that America might be in need of something at least as new and distinctive of her as the great business plants and concentrations that he and his fellow-magnates were, with such vivid immediate success and such ultimate bad consequences, making. So that the extensive and complicated university system of America remained essentially European, first upon the British pattern and then with an increasing German influence. To this day it clings to the medieval cap and gown, the degree-giving and medieval lecturing of the old world.

Dollar preoccupation was almost as effective in leaving unchallenged the ascendancy of Europe and European patterns in the world of thought and artistic creation. Boston, which had played a vigorous part in British intellectual life in colonial days, resented this acceptance of inferiority, but until well into the latter quarter of the nineteenth century the European ascendancy was tacitly admitted in the rest of America. Lowell might complain of a "certain air of condescension" in the visiting English of his time. This air of condescension had this much justification that in many strata of the American world it was accepted. There were insurgent spirits and many protests indeed, but the War of Independence only reached the realm of literary criticism towards the turn of the century, and then it came as a great shock to the British writers of my generation, who had taken the American tribute for granted. Today no young American writer would dream of sedulously imitating or indeed resembling a British model. And in many fields of thought, the new history and sociological speculation for example, individual minds broke into distinctive American methods. Some thirty odd years ago the American climate, by way of a protest, killed all the cherished ivy on those red-bricked colleges, but it did nothing further in the matter. To this day the shape of the knowledge organization and education, and particularly of the higher education, remains in precisely the same state of picturesque headlessness and material ineffectiveness as the older, natural-grown, European disorder of institutions. The erection of facsimile buildings, Magdalen Tower in Chicago, for example, is merely the extreme expression of this reverential attitude.

## AMERICAN MENTALITY

The United States, let alone the world, cannot carry on now with an unorganized mentality, a scattered higher education that has no power over the press or the common schools or political consciences. It produces no adequate civil service, no well-informed and easily co-operative administrators. It cannot compass any of the major problems before the nation. The resort of the undergraduate world to the realities of the playing fields is a sure indication of the unattractiveness of its array of subjects. They yell. Every university has a yell. And well may they yell and go wild and frantic in their stadiums, for their lives and their powers are being largely wasted.

Yet it is in America now that the clearest hope for a beginning of that World Brain resides. A country habituated to the rapid development of vast commercial and industrial enterprises must surely be capable of attempting an intellectual and educational enterprise beyond the imagination of men bred in smaller and more tradition-ridden communities. So far it has been impossible to awaken any influential and resourceful people to this patent, if unprecedented necessity. It is unhappily so novel that they seem afraid to realize how obvious it is and unavoidable. There is no time to lose about it. It is hard to guess what may happen when this abnormal phase of personal government by one inspired, insufficiently able man of genius comes to an end. There is no one to replace him and nothing to replace him. Nothing is being prepared. America may relapse in quite a little time into something as acephalous and incalculable as Russia.

And so I return to my refrain: "We need a World Brain," and to my insistence that the creation of a greater mental superstructure to reorient the mind of the world is an entirely practicable proposal.

At this point I imagine an angry critic interrupts. He has been skimming through this book—he wouldn't deign to read it or mark the course of its argument—looking for occasion for offense. And now he cries: "Who are you, Mr. Know-all, to tell us that all these splendid institutions, Harvard, Yale, Princeton, Columbia, Chicago, Johns Hopkins and a multitude of others, and abroad Oxford, Cambridge, Paris, London, Coimbra, Upsala, Tokio—one could count a thousand galaxies of clustering colleges and dreaming spires —and all these wise and good men, thousands of them, men of eminent learning, men of distinguished character, doctors, teachers, investigators, scholars, not one who is not in every respect a far better man than yourself, that all together they amount to nothing! that this great constellation, this veritable shining skyful of gifts and powers is not sufficient for the needs of the world today! that altogether it amounts to no more, scale for scale—what did you say?—than the brain of a horse! that it needs something far more powerful, some far vaster embodiment of knowledge and purpose—some queer fad of yours?"

To which I answer: What are they doing now? So far from lighting the world, the skies are so overcast that these starry constellations seem scarcely to be shining.

And far from being "Mr. Know-all," I am in helpless ignorance, in a sea of unconscious ignorance. There is one thing, and one thing only, I know, that you do not seem to know, and that is this—that neither you nor I know enough nor know the little that we do know well enough, to meet the needs of the world's occasions. Unless we do something about this ignorance of ours, this universal blinkered ignorance, we shall be overwhelmed, we shall destroy one another.

If only some small fraction of the still considerable wealth and energy of America could be turned not merely to a campaign against the ignorance of others but against its own far more dangerous ignorance; if only this absolute necessity for an organized World Brain, a gigantic but still possible super-university, set above all these admirable but ineffective scattered foundations to utilize and consolidate them, if only that could fire the imagination of a few energetic spirits; then the whole outlook of the human species might still be changed.

There is a last possibility to consider in this survey. Some such appeal as I am making may presently gather force, attract a measure, but an insufficient measure, of support and not enough critical attention. The thing may be tried, the effort may be made, and, as people say, it may fall into the wrong hands. Instead of a living World Brain we may have a sham World Brain. The effort may be made. Money may be forthcoming; the demand may grow. Something to look like a world encyclopædic organization may be brought into being, good enough to pacify most of the clamor, good enough for those people who say you cannot have everything at once—you must have a beginning. When embryonic tissue cannot build an organ it can still produce a cancer. We may have some large and plausible organization of platitudes, irrelevances and compromises, as adequate as an organization of knowledge as the old League of Nations was of world peace. There may be great academic comings and goings, ceremonies and solemn consecrations.

And at last something in the nature of Dr. Nicholas Murray Butler and President Grover Whalen will appear enthroned, side by side, organizers of the World Brain triumphant, the World Brain of Tomorrow, brooding profoundly over the unmitigated destiny of mankind.[1]

That may be. The history of most religions supports this possibility. There is nothing whatever between the stars and the atoms to show why the end of *Homo sapiens* should not be absurd as well as tragic. The price of human salvation is eternal vigilance, incessant fearless criticism and unrestricted wit. How can one tell beforehand whether that price will be forthcoming? Without unrestrained free speech and irreverence, how can we defeat the universal human tendency to be satisfied with and tolerant towards plausible, pretentious things? There can be no rest, no tactful acquiescences, no mental toleration, no enfeebling politeness, in the *Kulturkampf* ahead, if man is to escape the evils that close in upon him.

In the design of this book three primary themes interlace and pursue and develop each other. There is first, that invention and science have completely altered the material environment of human life. Next, that the disruptive driving-force of an excess of bored and unemployed young men, which must in some manner find relief, will probably shatter human life altogether under the new conditions. And thirdly, that the existing mental organization of our species is entirely insufficient to control the present situation, which nevertheless might, with an adequate effort, be controlled. These are the Change of Scale theme, the Youth Pressure theme and the World Brain theme. The first two create the

[1] Cf. *The Columbia Encyclopædia*.

problem to which the third indicates the only possible solution.

About the role of those young men; its cardinal importance is still not recognized plainly by sociologists, historians and writers of contemporary history. In practice, however, it is plainly apprehended, and a very considerable amount of propaganda to capture the imagination of this vital stratum is carried on, and particularly by the more aggressive contemporary states. They pursue their co-nationals abroad, and make strenuous efforts to win over opinion in neutral states and bring local conditions into parallelism with their own. Nazi patterns are being studied in South Africa, for example, and we have noted the Fascist disposition of General Chiang Kai Shek. There is a great totalitarian propaganda, and now, awakening and responding to it, there is counter-propaganda.

On the whole the totalitarians make the more exciting and attractive promises and give the brooding young man the most immediate prospect of authorized masterful activities. Official Great Britain pays the dole and encourages no presumptuous hopes. But in America and elsewhere there is a definitely anti-Fascist organization called the World Youth movement. This is a brotherhood and fundamentally a pacifist organization, a combination of a great number of more specialized associations, which attempts to bring the opinions and demands of the young for security from massacre and for employment, training, adult education, health culture and so forth, to bear upon governing and administrative bodies, and exert a critical, helpful and mediatory influence upon their social welfare work. It has the open support of both the President and his wife, more particularly of Mrs. Roosevelt, and it extends its liaison work into most of the so-called democracies—and Russia. Its activities vary with the country and occasion, but its general objective is to keep its young people busy with work of public importance, developing their capacity with use and experience. This World Youth movement claims to represent and affect the politico-social activities of a grand total of forty million adherents—under the age of thirty. Of these, twelve million are credited to Russia, though I cannot imagine how these figures are checked. It includes also a number of War Resisters whose ideas stop short at a repudiation of war. They will have nothing to do with war, but how human affairs are to be carried on in a warless world they do not trouble to think. Anyone else can bother about that, it seems, not they. They carry passive resistance to the pitch of know-nothingness. With a certain disapproval they offer us their bodies to be protected and their mouths to be fed.

I mention the World Youth Movement here, but I am quite unable to estimate its possibilities. It may fade out. It may play an important and increasing role in the consolidation of a new world order.

The President and Mrs. Roosevelt, though they seem acutely aware that a developing Youth Movement may play an important part in the political drama of tomorrow, have neither of them betrayed any consciousness of the immense intellectual reorientation of which the world is now in such urgent need. Their circumstances have never directed their attention to that. I doubt if these two fine, active minds have ever inquired how it is they know what they know and think as they do. Nor have they ever thought of what they might have been if they had grown up in an entirely different culture. They have the disposition of all politicians the world over to deal only with *made* opinion. They have never inquired how it is that opinion is made.

The only representative of Youth I have ever met who seemed to be aware that they were under-educated and improperly educated were some Burmans I met in Rangoon. "We are taught to be clerks in European-owned factories," they complained. "What we want is technical knowledge and the science of our own country and circumstances so as to give us a clear conception of our role in the world...."

Now that was saying something.[1]

---

[1] For a fuller factual and more hopeful analysis of the American process see C. A. and Mary R. Beard's *The Rise of American Civilization* and *America in Midpassage*. A characteristic statement of American notions is *Speaking of Change*, giving the ideas, attitudes and limitations of the late Edward A. Filene.

## 23

### THREE FACTORS IN EVERYONE

WE HAVE NOW EXPOSED, in stripped outline, the primary factors in world affairs at the present time. In all these matters I have written with the complete freedom of a biologically trained and uncontrolled observer. Sir Arthur Salter, for example, in his *Security. Can We Retrieve It?* (1939), writes with all the discretions and reserves of a responsible politician who has to think and speak within the conventions that I, in my entire irresponsibility, can repudiate and kick aside. His thoughts are capped and gowned and mine are stark. He has an air of scarcely recognizing the realities I assemble. Nevertheless, his intelligence and integrity are manifestly forcing him towards a conception of public policy and the human future essentially the same as those I have stated concisely and brutally here.[1]

The cultural summaries made in the preceding sections from § 11 onward may be offensive to many readers, if only because of their plainness, but they have been made with deliberation, they have been sustained when necessary by citation, and they will be much easier to run away from than to disprove. The political map is imposed upon these primary factors and more or less conditioned by them, very

[1] See *Note* 23A for a quotation from his *Epilogue.*

## THREE FACTORS IN EVERYONE

much as it is imposed upon a contoured physical map of the world. It entirely distorts the truth to attempt to reduce this complex struggle for existence to any left and right antagonism. At the maximum simplification we have still to distinguish three absolutely divergent trends in ourselves and in the world about us. Each of these trends has its variations, but these variations can be put very easily as species under one or other of these three genera. The divergence of the three main trends remains complete.

The first of these trends embodies the inveterate disposition of the normal man to accept his immediate circumstances as he finds them and make the best of them for himself. He sticks to the creed he is born to or to the alternative culture that gives him greater comfort. One might write, indeed, not merely the inveterate disposition of the normal man but the inveterate disposition of every normal living thing. For the ordinary animal the loss of the sense of security releases panic, flight, violence—vehement and usually quite unintelligent efforts to recover the confidence that has slipped away. It is only in the human animal, and probably it is only in the last two or three thousand years that there has been any disposition to look forward, even during a fairly prosperous social phase, beyond the prescribed social round, not only to anticipate and arrest danger but also to enlarge, enrich and alter life. There is a faint uneasiness. "Man looks before and after." For the first time in mental history the quality of reality is shifted from the present or from a past-present system to the future. Already in this book (§ 9) the idea of a rotation of values in time has been developed in reference to European thought in the past half-century and with an auto-vivisection of one particular sample. Now we are able to envisage that forced rotation of the mind as a world phenomenon.

Everywhere we note a natural, retrospective conservatism, and everywhere we have minds reluctantly and inadequately coming about and taking up the constructive challenge of the age. Such are the two main antagonistic trends in the mental life of the world today. The third trend goes neither backward nor forward; it is moral abandon. It is equally regardless of the reactionary passive peace desire and of the creative peace impulse. The manifest relapse of the world towards lawless warfare and recklessly destructive violence is due to the successful blocking of the road to the latter peace by the resistance of those who desire the continuance of the former. The deadlock between conservative instinct and creative readjustment releases the suppressed beast, the unqualified egotist in the species, from control. It can only be recalled to discipline for good and all by the complete triumph of the new peace over the old.

This triangular struggle is going on now not only in the human species as a whole but in every intelligent individual among us. It is the essential religious struggle of the time. In every one of us there is the disposition to acquiesce in the dear familiar values, faith, creed, patriotism, culture, amidst which we began. In every one there stirs the protest against a fatuous surrender to things plainly unstable and unsound; the protest and the creative desire even at the price of personal loss and injury. Moments come when we feel that we "must speak out." And there is the ever-recalcitrant egotism which lies in wait for every phase of perplexity, inducing us to abuse every confidence put in us, to snatch the profit and pleasure and personal glorification that offer themselves,

## THREE FACTORS IN EVERYONE

so that even leadership turns insensibly into a clamor for precedence, a jealous tyranny and the betrayal of all it set out to serve.

So it is we are all constituted. "Let him who thinketh he stand, take heed lest he fall."

# 24

## SUMMARY

THERE IS NO CREED, no way of living left in the world at all, that really meets the needs of the time.

When we come to look at them coolly and dispassionately, *all* the main religions, patriotic, moral and customary systems in which human beings are sheltering today, appear to be in a state of jostling and mutually destructive movement, like the houses and palaces and other buildings of some vast, sprawling city overtaken by a landslide. To the very last moment, in spite of falling rafters and bulging walls, men and women cling to the houses in which they were born and to the ways to which they have grown accustomed. At the most they scuttle into the house opposite or the house next door. They accuse each other of straining the partitions, overtaxing the material; they attack the people over the way for secret mining operations. They cannot believe such stresses can continue. The city is still sound enough, they say, if it is not too severely tried. At any pause in the wreckage they say "What did I tell you? It's all over. Now we can feel safe again," and when at last they realize the inevitability and universality of disaster, most of them have become too frantic to entertain the bare possibility of one

## SUMMARY 231

supreme engineering effort that might yet intercept those seeping waters that have released the whole mountainside to destruction.

Such a salvaging of the species is still just possible. That is as much as the most hopeful mind can say.

## 25

### IMPOSSIBILITY OF UTOPIANISM

IN A PREVIOUS SECTION (§ 10) I have given my reasons for and against believing that this creative world peace I have shown to be possible, will be achieved in time to save our species from disaster. I fluctuate, I admit, between at the best a cautious and qualified optimism and my persuasion of swiftly advancing, irretrievable disaster. Now let me assemble the probable experiences before our children in the event of such a conclusive frustration of democratic and progressive hope.

This is a much easier task than an attempt to forecast a progressive triumph. Upon that it would be possible to speculate only in the most general terms. What the human intelligence, no longer hag-rid, released from that abject fear of change that has restrained it through the ages, what the released and implemented creative imagination of thousands of millions of free and happily active individuals might achieve, is beyond any anticipating. At the utmost we can produce words like vacant frames and empty showcases, to indicate that undelivered wealth. We can talk of unhampered and unhurrying swiftness of realization, of universal variety, of abundance and balanced beauty. We are forced to take refuge as St. Paul did, when he evaded the greedy materialism of those who demanded a bodily resurrection from him, in "eye hath not seen nor ear heard, nor hath it entered into the heart of man to conceive" . . .

It is impossible to foretell what the liberated human mind may produce, but at least we can foretell one certain reaction to what is given here. There are those who cling with an obstinate willfulness to the persuasion that a unified world must be a uniform and stagnating world. It is ridiculous, but they manage to believe it. "Horrible monotony," they say, "stress and servitude. Bolshevik tyranny. Prigs' Paradise," and nothing will dissuade them.[1] Many, I am persuaded, feel an intense jealousy of the possibility of a state of affairs better and happier than their own. It is an intolerable thought for the greedier sort of mind that there should be any possible life finer than the one they live, a finer life that they will never share and which indeed they would be incapable of sharing. Their reaction to all forecasts and Utopias, possible or impossible, is self-protective hatred. They interrupt; they leap out with "That wouldn't suit *me*." As indeed it would not. How inevitable is that uncomfortable, protesting laugh: "I'm glad *I* shan't have to live in this dreadful, tidied-up, drab, *ordered* world of yours."

The congratulations are mutual. I won't even ask you, Madam, to read in your newspaper between the social and the sporting columns and mark how brightly and swiftly you and your kind drive down towards your destiny.

On the other hand, mankind in defeat and decadence involves no great probabilities of mental novelty. There is nothing to alarm your self-complacency in that. It is the

[1] See, for example, Aldous Huxley's *Brave New World*.

world we live in now, only a little farther on and a little more so. We need not speculate outside the traditional, limited, human stuff, that dear old "unchanging human nature" of the past twenty or thirty thousand years. And to that we will now apply ourselves.

## 26

### DECADENT WORLD

IT WAS BECOMING EVIDENT to everyone that the present state of affairs could not continue. The greater part of mankind was living in the immediate fear of sudden, undeclared war. At any time, by night or day, with less than an hour's notice, the screaming sirens and the high explosive and incendiary bombs were expected to burst about us. Every other occupation was subordinated to the ill-conceived exigencies of air-raid precautions, and an ever-increasing proportion of our human and material resources was pouring into military preparations. Almost every intelligent human being and every township and community in Eur-Asia was in a state of mental tension which was rapidly approaching the breaking-point. Suicides were increasing. Lucid thinking became offensive and intolerable. People attacked and persecuted one another on flimsy excuses. Because of the limited and distorted idea systems in which they are living, they were, as we have seen in §§ 11 to 22, incapable of setting about the necessary readjustments of relationship. We have dismissed any such outbreak of sanity, therefore, as improbable. There is no basis on which it can start. There will be no world unification, because our species is too distraught and divided for anything of the sort.

What seems much more likely is a lapse into actual warfare, red war, on a planetary scale. This will not be a clearly conceived war carried out with the intention of establishing a world peace. Governments will pretend it is that, but fundamentally it will be a fit of frantic violence with no rational objective whatever. The first offensive was just as likely to come from the so-called "democratic" as from the "dictator" side.

As we have shown quite clearly by an appeal to manifest facts, the threefold forces making for conflict are to be found busily active in every existing human community —the evil patriotic and religious traditions, the horribly magnified weapons, the relative excess of unemployed young men—but the states where the pressure of these forces, because they were most pent up, has produced its maximum effect in menace and belligerent gestures, will be marked as the aggressor states. They will be assailed by a loose alliance of incongruous countries animated by the diverse motive systems we have scrutinized, and agreed only upon the need of suppressing these desperado nations. The ensuing war is likely to be briefer but far more violently destructive than the previous world war, because while that war began at a level of equipment which permitted a steady increase in the supply of munitions almost to the end when the losers collapsed through material and moral exhaustion, the combatants this time start from the beginning at something like a maximum of armament, and will reach the breaking-point much earlier. Staying power will decide the formal victory, which is less likely to be decisive even than the surrender of the eleventh of November, 1918.

## DECADENT WORLD

The material and moral destruction of the actual warfare will certainly be enormous. The population stratum of military age will be largely killed, mutilated, poisoned or mentally unbalanced, and after it, will come a generation or so, which has been more and more undernourished, undereducated, demoralized and mentally distorted, as the concentration upon preparation (guns for butter) and the actual stress, noise and disorder of the conflict, have made a normal growth impossible for them. Vast resources of power will have been wasted for good and all, and the land and the sea bottom will be littered with smashed-up aeroplanes, shattered tanks, twisted railway trucks, burnt-out aerodromes and a great abundance of sunken ships and stores. Exoduses of population hardly less frightful than battle routs will have dislocated all sanitary balances, and famine and its follower, pestilence, will have swept the world. Even the influenza epidemic which followed the previous Great War killed more people than were actually slain in battle. This time the sanitary disorganization will certainly be much greater and the possibilities of morbid infections far more various. Probably there will be a deliberate spraying of disease germs to assist this more natural mischief. There will have been much gratuitous bombing of cities. There will have been a great burning and smashing-up of human habitations which no one will have had energy to replace, and such a destruction of beautiful buildings, works of art and irreplaceable loveliness of all sorts, as will make the feats of the Huns and Vandals seem mere boyish mischief. All that lies plainly ahead.

And when at last one side admits defeat, and peace is

proclaimed upon the world battlefield, what will be the situation? The defeated will be treated as the incurably guilty parties. If that were so, if there were incurably malignant peoples, then the wholesome thing to do would be to massacre them carefully and completely. Mankind will balk at that.

Instead of any such biologically conclusive settlement, there will be, once again, a punitive peace. The victors, to the best of their ability, will make the losers pay. The losers will be quite unable to pay. Further punitive measures will then become necessary. Modern war is a very impartial process, and the victors will probably have suffered quite as much and even more material and social devastation than the vanquished. They will be in no mind for generosity. No country in the world, even those that have preserved a technical neutrality, alert under arms, will emerge from the storm at anything like the level of civilization at which it stands today. There will be less freedom of speech, less opportunity to speak freely, far more fear and far more danger of frantic mass impulses.

In §§ 11 to 22 there has been an attempt to estimate the general trend of the main idea systems of the world. Here we may recapitulate the conclusions to which that survey points. What is going on now?

A very considerable festering of minds is no doubt occurring. People are reading and thinking feverishly but they are often thinking wrong and with an assisted wrong-headedness. Patriotic and religious teachings surround them, and subtle and insidiously mischievous suggestions. The arts of propaganda in enemy countries improve rapidly. There is no country in the world where enemies are not sowing tares

## DECADENT WORLD

with constantly increasing effectiveness. Every form of discontent is fomented with a skill and energy worthy of a better cause. The suggestions of desperate and destructive revolt that men may fear to whisper to their neighbors, will come to them from abroad.

We have seen that the break-up of the British Imperial system in face of a complex of insurrectionary movements, troubles on which the sun will never set, has a high degree of probability. The conflict of the new Nazi religion with Catholicism is plain and open, we have studied it in the ingenuous speculations of Mr. Teeling, and beneath the surface of most of the established systems of today, some queer development of social dissent is latent. The present ebb of communism is no end to insurrectionary class war. It is muttering vaguely, it may be unorganized and criminal, but it will be none the less socially destructive. We have noted the waning charm of the Italian dictatorship and the lamentable tendency of original sin to emerge as murder and fanatical cruelty under the very shadow of obscurantist Christian teaching. Where Spanish and Portuguese are spoken the pronunciamento flourishes with undiminished vitality.

America has a transitory unity and stability under the protean aspects of the New Deal, but no one knows what will follow when the extremely personal direction of Franklin Roosevelt ceases. There may be a heavily financed drive to put back the New Deal and return to a hard-faced business individualism. Big business has used some rough methods in the past and may resort to still rougher methods again—in an atmosphere that has become much less tolerant of the old forms of firmness. Not without reason do Americans talk of their Bourbons. That once unorganized alien labor has become assimilated and unified and more capable of meeting pseudo-legal violence with extra-legal violence. The country that produced Franklin Roosevelt also produced at the same time Huey Long and an unprecedented regime of gangster terrorism. And in the same period came the revival and the suppression of the intimidations of the Ku Klux Klan. Things have a way of beginning in America, running large and rank, and then coming suddenly to an end. This applies to evil and hopeful things alike. Everything may occur in some part of the United States or another, and the country may still retain an apparent unity. With a strong personality the White House may concentrate the nation, as it were, into one mind; with a less vigorous head that federal unification relaxes and the continental expanse is revealed as a miscellany of divergent issues. War and Roosevelt might impose a temporary national personality upon the United States that would vanish again in a subsequent reaction, giving place to a state of affairs as incoherent and variegated as Europe. The apparent solidarity of the United States may be as personal as any dictatorship; it may be accidental and not essential.

The question of what will come after Roosevelt opens a vista of localized possibilities varying between dull conflict, boss rule and chaotic violence, and the corresponding question of what will come after Stalin opens up not a vista but darkness. We have weighed up the uncertainties of China and Japan, and there too there is no assurance of stability and many intimations of degenerative revolution. A Japanese collapse would probably disintegrate China again, for nothing but patriotism holds China together.

So we have left as the main factors in the settlement after

## DECADENT WORLD 241

the second world war, a patchwork of staggering governments ruling over a welter of steadily increasing social disorganization. The settlement after the next world war will be only a prelude to further conflict. Informal warfare will succeed the formal struggle. What else can happen? Victors and vanquished will go to pieces and rearrange themselves. There is no body of ideas in existence, no tradition or frame of a world law to which an appeal can be made, that can carry on the shattered, mentally and morally overstrained, but still heavily armed combatants to any sort of world synthesis. The seizures and pronunciamentos that followed the Treaty of Versailles will recur more abundantly and on a more sustained and uncontrollable scale.

Since any new synthesis is improbable, the names of the existing main political systems are likely to continue long after they have lost any real authority, just as the idea of the Empire prevailed among the barbarians in the Dark Ages. The Union Jack, the Swastika, the Cross, or the Stars and Stripes may still float over a thousand dissociated gangs and tribes, claiming its authority, just as the Roman Eagle survived as a legally dominating reality in man's imaginations, side by side with the Church, long after Rome was sacked.

Now it may be thought that so much political and social dissolution may mean an ebb of invention and a break-up of the industrial organizations that supply the destructive apparatus which is smashing up the existing order so rapidly and uncontrollably. The human process will go back, it may be fancied, to a mechanically feeble barbarism, and a new system of expanding states may finally reconstruct civilization. It will be the Dark Ages over again, a planetary instead of a merely European Dark Ages. *Homo sapiens* will be given a second opportunity. There will be a return to primitive home-made weapons, non-mechanical transport, a new age if not of innocence yet of illiteracy, and slow, feeble and less lethal mischiefs will return to the world. But history never repeats itself, ecological processes are irreversible, and there are many considerations that make it improbable that the new barbarism which is coming upon us will have even a material resemblance to the barbarism of sixteen centuries ago. It will be much tougher, with a livelier and wickeder intelligence, and it will retain a far more destructive equipment.

Because it is proving impossible to assemble and organize knowledge and sane ideas for the establishment of a world civilization, it does not follow that knowledge already scattered about the earth will be destroyed. It may become generally inaccessible and secret, but it may continue available in workable fragments to a number of enterprising people. A vast store of metallurgical and industrial technique was completely lost with the downfall of the Roman Empire,[1] but then the record of principles and processes was very flimsy and vulnerable. Many technical secrets were never written at all and none were printed. Even down to the past century that sort of thing went on; a number of the processes in Wedgwood's china factory, for example, were transmitted verbally from one worker to another. Some of the older men carried secrets with them to the grave, and an analytical chemist had to be called in and the processes laboriously rediscovered before the firm could go on producing its characteristic wares. That was a survival of old-

---

[1] Rendered rather vividly in George Gissing's *Veranilda*.

world methods. Under such conditions the old techniques disappeared in a generation or so. But nowadays scientific and technical knowledge is embodied in so huge a number of printed and widely distributed publications, the body of people in contact with those records is so large and varied, that even in a world of deepening and extensive disorder, it will still be possible to assemble knots and groups of men capable of carrying on the production of most of the lethal devices now in use. Postal and railway organization may go to pieces, newspapers disappear, roads become impassable and gas supply, drainage, and public lighting cease, because such things depend upon a widespread social co-operation, and still there may be radio transmission, aeroplanes and high explosives, which do not demand anything like the same general participation.

It does not follow that mechanisms and contrivances will disappear in reverse order to that in which they appeared. It may have taken long years of research and the contribution of thousands of scientific workers to discover an explosive or a poison, but when that has been attained only a recipe and material are needed for its production. It has become a part of "our human heritage."

This is evident for example in the steady increase of bomb-making and bomb-throwing in the world. It is a growing feature of the normal social life. Every morning now we read in our newspapers of the young braves of the Irish Republican Army throwing their cheap but effective bombs in Great Britain, the Jew boys and the Arab boys bomb each other with ever-increasing zeal and bloodier results, bomb outrages comment on the new regime in Spain, they multiply in India, in the occupied areas of

China. In a world of deepening misunderstandings and grievances, there is no reason to doubt that they will become as common as road accidents and as little thought of, a part of the normal give and take of politics. People will harden their hearts to their consequences until the bomb comes to themselves, and then their enlightenment will be too late.

The world emerging from the next great war, then, will be a tougher world, more disunited than ever, abounding still more in concealed aims and secret preparations and the fears and suspicions they engender. What else can it be? The open forum of the scientific world will have disappeared and the suggestion of any cosmopolitan ideas will have been suppressed, as a weakening of combatant morale. In every country. For the neutral powers, if any remain, will still have had to be mentally as well as materially "prepared." Human beings who can do nothing else to gratify their craving to exercise power, love to suppress and help suppression.

No doubt great numbers of people will have felt the irrational evil of all this shrinking of thought into strategic holes and corners, but they will have had less and less opportunity of getting together, or even clearing up their own minds sufficiently to take effective action. Many of them, under the stress of their conscious helplessness, will lapse into mystical religiosity, will refuse to bear children, will resort to suicide or the quasi-suicide of non-resistance. Many will take refuge in opiates. The Japanese are doing their utmost to spread the use of opium and heroin among the Chinese, and they will probably succeed in affecting their own troops also. The ideas and expedients of birth

## DECADENT WORLD

control, now they have spread about the earth, will not be easily forgotten.

More and more will the world be for the tough, for the secretive, the treacherous and ruthless. Cities will be dangerous labyrinths and the countryside an exposure to attack. Ever and again some group or some individual by luck or cunning may achieve a certain width of conquest and establish a peace of terror. Subservient millions may rejoice then for awhile that at last strong government has come back to the world. They will accept an imposed religion, a last revival of Christianity à la Franco perhaps, or of that "clean" Nazi creed, or something on the evangelical lines General Chiang Kai Shek seems to favor; they will observe a dictated morality and a mutual censorship. Any intellectual revival is improbable. This light of free science will have sunken and gone out long since; what remains of technical knowledge will be in the safe hands of properly ordained men. The first thing a youth attracted to mechanical or medical knowledge will do, will be to take orders and put himself under safe direction. History will have shriveled down to the Creator myth again, but the popular imagination will be titillated and appalled by a dim and dying tradition of a former age, our age, of sinful knowledge, of lawless indulgence, of unconsecrated loves, of a terrible disrespect for customs and taboos and sacrifices and priests, that brought great misfortunes upon mankind. A new "World before the Flood" it will be.

A few secret doubters may exist, bookish, silent, hinting and whispering men—*men,* for a more "wholesome" use of womankind will leave women little time for reading—

who will pore guiltily over the unfulfilled promises of a golden age to come, in the old books which men wrote when they still had pride and hope. There may be some wistful whisperings, some weak attempts at a new Freemasonry. But the necessary adaptation of human thought to turn the tide of decadence is something too wide and open in its nature to be brought about by any sort of secret organization. What can be done by timid men who are forced to squeak and scamper like mice behind the arras?

Art may have an Indian summer. The dictator may even build some fine buildings—for most of them build—monasteries, cathedrals, palaces, before he passes. There may be portrait painting and portrait pieces of an ennobling type, glorified history, an effort at a technically lower level to recall the Venetian bravura of Titian, Tintoretto and Paul Veronese. At any rate we shall not live to see that last Art Age. Then, because there will be no correction for the material stresses of a static system, the darkness will close in again. There will be peasant revolts, an exhausting war or dynastic trouble. So human affairs have gone in the past, and so, without any fundamental change in human mentality, they must continue to go, so long as they go on at all.

The coming barbarism will differ from the former barbarism by its greater powers of terror, urgency and destruction, and by its greater rapidity of wastage. What other difference can there be without a mental renascence? The average life will be steadily diminishing, health will be deteriorating. The viruses and pestilential germs will resume their experiments in variation, and new blotches and infections will give scope for pious resignation and turn men's hearts again towards a better world beyond the stars. There will be a last crop of saints and devotees. Mankind which began in a cave and behind a windbreak will end in the disease-soaked ruins of a slum. What else can happen? What other turn can destiny take?

If *Homo sapiens* is such a fool that he cannot realize what is before him now and set himself urgently to save the situation while there is still some light, some freedom of thought and speech, some freedom of movement and action left in the world, can there be the slightest hope that in fifty or a hundred years hence, after he has been through two or three generations of accentuated fear, cruelty and relentless individual frustration, with ever diminishing opportunity of apprehending the real nature of his troubles, he will be collectively any less of a fool? Why should he undergo a magic change when all the forces, within him as without, are plainly set against it?

There is no reason whatever to believe that the order of nature has any greater bias in favor of man than it had in favor of the icthyosaur or the pterodactyl. In spite of all my disposition to a brave looking optimism, I perceive that now the universe is bored with him, in turning a hard face to him, and I see him being carried less and less intelligently and more and more rapidly, suffering as every ill-adapted creature must suffer in gross and detail, along the stream of fate to degradation, suffering and death.

That, compactly, is the human outlook, the only possible alternative to the willful and strenuous adaptation by re-education of our species now—forthwith—that I am urging in this book. Adapt or perish, that is and always has been the implacable law of life for all its children. Either the human imagination and the human will to live, rises to the plain necessity of our case, and a renascent *Homo sapiens* struggles on to a new, a harder and a happier world dominion, or he blunders down the slopes of failure through a series of unhappy phases, in the wake of all the monster reptiles and beasts that have flourished and lorded it on the earth before him, to his ultimate extinction. Either life is just beginning for him or it is drawing very rapidly to its close. This is no guess that is put before you, no fantasy; it is a plain and reasoned assembling of known facts in their natural order and relationship. It faces you. Meet it or shirk it, this is the present outlook for mankind.

**THE END**

# NOTES

*Note* 4A. A shrinkage of the gross population, one may note, under the new conditions, though it foreshadows an ultimate biological defeat, does not in itself compensate for that superfluity of unemployed and dangerously restless young men stressed in the preceding paragraphs. It does nothing to stabilize the community. Not merely increased productivity per head due to technical progress but also the prolonged activity of skilled older people will still be diminishing employment and the young man's prospects of normal assuagement. A falling birth rate or for that matter a rising one is no relief for that primary social tension, which is essentially a matter of proportion and not of scale. An island community of a few hundred people will still be unstable if it includes a few dozen young men with nothing definite to do.

*Note* 4B. Semaphore signaling systems seem only to have been invented in the Napoleonic period, though it is remarkable they were not attempted in the great Empires of Egypt, Persia, China and Rome.

*Note* 6A. It is true that in Great Britain there are certain organizations, the Plebs League, for instance, and the Workers' Educational Association, which owe their existence to the realization that the traditional education, meeting as it does the requirements for upper and middle class survival, may not be entirely adequate for the needs of an awakening democracy. But in practice there is little of the interrogative and creative spirit of science in the work of these quasi-rebel bodies. A rash conceit of finality pervades them. One need only turn over the pages of *Plebs* to realize the glib, trite omniscience of its attitude. The aim throughout is not knowledge but equipment for the political class war; it is to assemble and supply predigested controversial material for the Labor politician (research!), prepare and train "speakers" for the Labor cause, and sustain the profound satisfaction of its clientele in such education as they have already derived from the general atmosphere of their upbringing. At a Royal Society Dinner one can stand up and say "We are all self-confessed ignorant men, our common aim is inquiry and better knowledge; we want to know, and that is why we are here together." But that sort of thing would provoke either indignation or derision in the Little Bethel of a workers' educational gathering. They have the Gospel; they know. Labor is going to take over things and the millennium will ensue. The Plebs League, it seems, has a doctrinal feud with the kindred Communist Party; I cannot understand why. It preaches practically the same stuff. No seminary for the missionaries of some eccentric sect was ever more specialized and narrow-minded.

*Note* 7A. There is a very full and well-illustrated Italian (Fascist) Encyclopædia—one of the many evidences of the higher mental level of the Fascist as compared with the Nazi regime—but I have never seen any competent examination of this work in any English, American or French review. I have no idea of what this attractive-looking publication gives, what it conceals, what it may suggest or misrepresent, and short of learning Italian and reading it through I do not see how I can find out. No university professor anywhere in the world seems to have bothered yet to put a research student or so on to this task. But why should he care? Why on earth should he care? It would be infringing on journalism. It would be vulgar. There is always something more to be done in the best academic tradition about the probable sex life of Leonardo da Vinci or the personal resentments of Dante, which will touch no current controversial issue and still satisfy the highest standards of academic erudition.

*Note* 9A. See Lord David Davies, *The Problem of the Twentieth Century* (1930), *Suicide or Sanity* (1932) and various publications of the New Commonwealth Society.

*Note* 9B. Dr. John Beattie Crozier, 1849-1921. Author of *The Religion of the Future* (1880) and *A History of Intellectual Development* (1897-1901).

## NOTES 251

*Note* 9c. "The world-wide English language is destined, I think, to serve as the primary medium in this renascence of the human spirit. Unquestionably that renascence must ultimately be cosmopolitan, but to begin with it is likely to find its fullest and most lucid expression in one or the other, or maybe one or two, of the existing thought and language systems in the world. What are they? What other systems are there? There is the Latin cultural group expressing itself in French, Italian and Spanish. In the past French has been the common medium, but it is by no means certain that it will remain so as intellectual suppression progresses in Italy and Spain. Then there is the great Slavonic sprawl whose medium of expression is Russian. There is the German system and, last and most widespread and convenient of all, there is the English-speaking network. I want to point out to you that for the next few decades at any rate, the burthen and responsibility for human mental progress or human mental failure will rest principally upon the series of communities using the English tongue either as a mother tongue or as a cultural language. It is becoming the *lingua franca* of the so-called "democracies." Matters may change later, but that is the present state of affairs. These communities are far more free to discuss, learn and publish than any other people in the world.

Germany as an organized country has, for a time at least, withdrawn herself from any claim to a share in the moral or intellectual leadership of the world. The burning of the books by the Nazis was a symbolical act of detachment from the free mentality of mankind. The expulsion of such men of science as Einstein and Freud, and the assertion of the racial hallucinations of Hitler in place of established ethnology, were practical demonstrations of the same withdrawal. Dogmatic nationalism has stamped upon science and free thought and the German mind and retired into itself. And so too has the Russian. Before the Great War, the Russian language and literature were the medium for civilized thought not only throughout Russia but all over the Slavonic-speaking world of southwest Europe. In the summer of 1938, just before the destruction of Czechoslovakia, I took part in a small conference upon Slavonic culture in Prague. It was attended by representatives of all the Slav-speaking countries except Poland, and I found that everyone in that meeting spoke and liked speaking Russian. But the present Russian government has seen fit to sterilize this Russian influence by a systematic suppression of free speech, free discussion and free publication. For all practical purposes this leaves only the French- and English-speaking systems. The French intelligence at its best is lucid, brave and enterprising, still finer I think in its quality than any other in the world, but it works upon a much narrower base than the English. The very precision of French deprives it of an amplitude of expression of which English is capable. So we come to the conclusion that if the human race is not to go on slipping down towards a bottomless pit of wars, conquests and exterminations, it must be through the rapid and zealous expansion and reorganization of the intellectual and education organizations of the English-speaking communities.

But let me make it clear that when I say English-speaking, I say it without any shadow of political propaganda, Anglo-Saxon radicalism, dear-old-Englandism, British imperialism or any shallow-witted stuff of that sort. I am thinking of the things our language carries, and can carry, and not of our contemporary "culture." And I think of a flexible language expanding to meet every fresh need. English is a very adaptable language; it borrows and assimilates words and idioms very freely; and when I speak of the English of the future, I have in mind something much more copious and powerful than the "correct English" of the academic scholars. It can already narrow down to Basic or expand to express a thousand delicate shades of meaning. I think of it as stripped of any remaining idiomatic complications with a reformed spelling and a continually expanding vocabulary.

Even now English brings together into one creative fermentation a vast diversity of peoples, from the Maori to the Eskimos; it enables an educated Indian to talk to an educated Norwegian or an educated West African Negro. It can bring all the thought and learning of the world within their understanding, as no other language can do. It translates everything of importance in every other

# NOTES 253

language under the sun. Its center of gravity is now the United States of America, but every several community which participates in its free exchanges contributes its distinctive experiences. See, for example, how the mental world of Australasia receives practically everything that America or Britain can give it, and in return produces great men of science, brilliant artists, writers, thinkers, . . . (Adapted from the Canberra lecture on *The Role of English in the Development of the World Mind*.)

*Note* 10A. While I was working on this chapter a little friend of mine who draws rather cleverly sent me a card to wish me a Happy Easter. Below that she had drawn two chicks emerging from their eggs with their little heads in gas masks over the legend "Be Prepared." I find my little niece's jest rather a grim one. But maybe there is an idea in that, a topical touch, for the Nativities they will be setting up next Christmas in bomb-devastated Madrid, now that Catholicism has waded through blood to its own again. It would be a halfhearted incarnation that did not fully share the anxieties and precautions of our distressful life.

*Note* 10B. Since the § 10 was first drafted, a very revolutionary device has come to hand in Major Muir's invention of the "air mine." This is a balloon-sustained mine which can be set adrift in the air at any level, and which will drift before the wind until it contacts with a plane and destroys it. It is too small to be seen and avoided. It can be timed to keep the air for a definite time, a day or a week or so, and then explode and come down. These air mines are cheap to produce and they could be made quickly and released in enormous quantities. So long as they were up they would make the air impossible for any sort of air transport, civil or military; they would in fact for the time being eliminate the air altogether. I have consulted several authorities in this matter, and they agree upon its entire practicability. But obviously there are considerable obstacles to its being properly tried out. The combatant air forces detest the idea. Still there we have the possibility of putting the air completely out of action whenever we wish it, and of restoring war to its ancient and slower two dimensions.

*Note* 11A. It is the practice of those who find the results of scientific inquiry unpalatable, to stigmatize such statements as we have assembled here as "cocksure" and declare them as dogmatic as any other dogmas. They will make it a personal matter if possible, as though I individually had made it all up, or got it wrong, and was being rather absurd about it. And then "Yah!", and they think no more about these uncongenial things. But I am no more responsible for the facts in this book than a telegraph messenger is for the cable he brings, I have been simply gathering up undisputed statements, and they remain intact, however brilliantly I can be discredited personally.

Alternatively these recalcitrant spirits will have it that it is science which is "cocksure." That is a flat misrepresentation of the scientific spirit. Experimental science, natural science—which is what everyone understands by "science" nowadays,—is never assured and final. That is where it differs from all other established systems of belief, and that is why I speak of it throughout this book as a new thing in the development of human mentality, new within the past century or so. The true symbol of natural science is a note of interrogation. A better name would be research. It questions until some false assumption is laid bare or destroyed. It tries out and rejects or accepts. And still it questions. It is rare that it reverses its carefully tested conclusions —it is another defensive invention that "Science is always contradicting itself"—but continually it advances beyond these conclusions and restates with increasing precision and enrichment. The utmost the man of science says to the religious dogmatist is "In view of this and that, your general statement is unsound," or, "In view of this and that it must be untrue."

*Note* 11B. "The number of one's ancestors increases as we look back in time. Disregarding the chances of intermarriage, each one of us had two parents, four grandparents, eight great-grandparents, and so on backward, until very soon, in less than fifty generations, we should find that, but for the qualification introduced, we should have all the earth's inhabitants of that time as our progenitors. For a hundred generations it must hold absolutely true, that everyone of

# NOTES

that time who has issue living now is ancestral to all of us. That brings the thing quite within the historical period. There is not a palæolithic or neolithic relic that is not a family relic for every soul alive. The blood in our veins has handled it."

From H. G. Wells. *First and Last Things,* "The Being of Mankind."

There are, however, certain qualifications to be made to this statement of our common ancestry if it is to pass unchallenged. In every generation there is an elimination of half the genetic elements. The individual is not a mixture of the total ancestry of his four grandparents. He is a compound of a quarter of their genes. And in addition he may be a mutation. Genes are transmitted in associated groups, but these groups fall infinitely short of carrying a complete personality. They carry traits, but the traits are carried separately. In so-and-so we may remark this and that trait of his Grandfather William but they are mixed with traits from other progenitors; the practical reappearance of Grandfather William is a mathematical improbability verging on the impossible. Of all this and how there are recessive characteristics masked by dominant ones, but capable of reappearing in offspring, the reader will find a clear and full account in *The Science of Life.*

A common ancestry does not therefore involve a common physiognomy, and at any time an individual or a type may turn up in which some once prevalent type virtually reappears. Mr. George Bernard Shaw, for example, is a very exceptional person today, but Etruscan tombs and potsherds reveal a departed world of quasi-George Bernard Shaws. There are quasi-Cromagnards in La Dordogne and the Canary Isles today. Certain regions, certain climates, seem to attract and favor their own special types and tend to revive them. That all English people are descended from William the Conqueror and most of the population of the earth from Abraham, implies brotherhood indeed, but not uniformity. The fact that if humanity survives so long, everyone alive will be the descendant of every fertile individual among us today exposes the absurdities of family and national pride, but it does not mean that the dance of the genes will not give us an incessantly restored human variety, in which every individual will be consciously or unconsciously seeking the region, the occupation and the associates most congenial to his make-up.

*Note* 12A. Some of those who, in spite of much subsequent enlightenment, still cling, out of natural affection and association, to traditions of their home and upbringing that have become a dear and necessary part of themselves, take refuge, I know, in the plea that the idea of the Chosen People has become altogether spiritualized, that they are now segregated not for an ultimate conquest but for a mission. Their mission is to serve and exalt all mankind.

There is moreover another line of sublimation with a bolder appeal, and that is the line taken by that great neglected genius, David Lubin, the founder of the International Institute of Agriculture in Rome. His Israel was indeed an Israel with a mission, but then he claimed everyone who participated in constructive work as one of the elect. To Lubin I was an honorary Israelite.

"But why then call it Israel?" I protested.

This sort of transfiguration of the objectives of the Chosen People is all very well in apologetic discussion, but there is nothing to sustain it in the normal ceremony and practice and teaching of the cult, which remains a narrow and troublesome nationalism. Let these sublimators repudiate the Bible and the Promise and say what they mean plainly. Then we shall be better able to believe in their assertions of an exalted inaggressive modernization.

*Note* 12B. Louis Golding (in *The Jewish Problem*) argues that anti-Judaism is due to the fact that the Jews cried "Crucify him," when Jesus came before Pilate. Jesus, as everybody knows, was crucified (a particularly Roman method of execution) not by the Jews but by the Roman Pontius Pilate. Countless people who criticize the Jews today are extremely impartial about the Crucifixion, and I find it difficult to believe that Mr. Golding, who, I presume, is himself a product of orthodox Jewish education, is so entirely unaware of the effect of this Chosen People cult upon the outside world as he seems to be. He ignores it absolutely.

Browne also, refusing to face that primary issue, accounts for the unpopularity of the Jewish community in an entirely different

# NOTES

manner. He theorizes brilliantly about Jews being urban while non-Jews are rustic. Certainly the Semitic-speakers were prevalently urban in the first century B.C. The balance, says he, must be corrected and all will be well. So the Jew, he decides (1935) had better go to Palestine and dig himself out of his troubles. Both writers then launch out into an account of the great intellectual superiority of Jews to Gentiles, wholesome rather than ingratiating reading for a puffed up Gentile, and cite a string of names, Sigmund Freud, for instance, and Einstein and so on, who are as a matter of fact no more orthodox Jews than I am. They are citizens of the world, they work for all mankind. Even now Freud is busy, he tells me, in a patient analysis of the legend of Moses. Moses, he concludes, was an Egyptian! His monotheism was Akhnaton's sun worship. (*Moses and Monotheism*.)

Both Golding and Browne are typical of a vast literature on the Jewish question. There is no need to multiply instances. Neither, I think, realizes quite clearly what it is that encompasses them, because they are themselves enveloped in it. They accept this taught and cultivated idea system, this ex-religious bias, this artificial solidarity I am arraigning, as though it was in the nature of things and could not be prevented, and thence they wander off into a limitless jungle of controversial irrelevances, of the rights and wrongs of ancient hates, misunderstandings, persecutions and reprisals, to which there can be no conclusion.

But the eloquent and emotional Mr. Josef Kastein, who dedicates his *History and Destiny of the Jews* quite incongruously to the entirely unorthodox Einstein, concludes his *Jews in Germany* with the real irreconcilable note:

". . . we were once in Egypt. Already we have compelled a Pharaoh to set us free. We have outlasted the Pyramids. We shall outlast the denials of all those who surround us."

As a matter of fact the Pyramids were there a long time before the Jews.

I reiterate that the whole scheme and purport of this book is to insist upon the supreme decisive importance of what in § 4 I have called the mental superstructure of the human animal. The reconstruction of its idea system is its only practicable method of adaptation, and here is an idea system that resists and evades reconstruction very obstinately. In §§ 8 and 9 I have assembled and summarized the nature of the great intellectual effort which is needed if our species is to adjust itself to the terrific new conditions that have risen about it. The Jewish conflict disregards this, cuts athwart it, arrests and prevents it, like a noisy quarrel in a laboratory. All the countervailing evil in the world cannot make a bad tradition a good one. Killing or ill-treating a man does not put him in the wrong, but also, we have to remember, and that is not so easy for the liberal-minded, it does not put him in the right. The idea of the solidarity of the Chosen People, evade it or not, remains the fundamental Jewish idea, and this fundamental Jewish idea, like any other nationalism, is an offense against the unity of mankind.

*Note* 12c. Persecution mania is a well-known form of insanity. With certain variations of phrase and form, due to the current ideas of the period, it presents an almost stereotyped pattern through the ages. Formerly it was usually witches and warlocks who were supposed to be at the root of the matter. Anyone odd, anyone different, came under suspicion, old crones and afflicted and odd-looking men were distrusted, and very often the suspects caught a touch of the infection and tried doing the things they learnt were so potent. Multitudes of sorcerers have confessed, under no great duress, to impossible crimes. They brewed potions, stuck pins in wax images, cast spells, sent familiar spirits to gibber and creep and whisper in the night.

Madness like everything else moves with the times; it clothes itself in new fashions while remaining essentially the same. Nowadays the witches have become "Occult Powers." They use hypnotism, electricity, infections (Pah!), they radio voices making threats and evil suggestions. Every prominent publicist continually gets letters from sufferers with this type of obsession. Such delusions may easily make the patient a danger to himself and others, and then he is "certified" and taken care of. But in times of social movement and stress this disorder may become contagious, witness the witch mania of the early seventeenth century. It is then more difficult to deal with.

# NOTES

Like a dark shadow to the rational objections that can be made to the in-and-out double nationalism of the Jews, there is a sustained campaign of sinister suggestion with a considerable literature of its own.

Some years ago four or five books written by Mrs. Nesta Webster attracted considerable attention. She is a very competent writer and so sound a Christian, of a faith so uncritical, that she is quite unable to understand that many honest people find a vast amount of Christian doctrine impossible. How impossible, I have sought to show in §§ 13 and 14. To her there is nothing good except in Christianity, and this is so obvious to her that any objection to the faith seems necessarily part of some diabolically hatched conspiracy. She has set herself with the greatest industry to trace and link together the long-drawn succession of Cabalists, Gnostics, Manichæans, the Old Man of the Mountains, Knight Templars, Satanists, Rosicrucians, Illuminati, Freemasons, Rousseau, Voltaire, Cagliostro, Madame Blavatsky, Mrs. Besant, Trade Unions, Anarchists, Socialists, Theosophists, Communists, Those Bolsheviks, a frightful horde all plotting and getting hold of power and handing it on and doing down Christianity and the Christian life. Her books are written with conviction enough to make one look under the bed at nights. She has never quite committed herself to those famous forged *Protocols of the Elders of Zion* which were published as the articles of association so to speak of that world conspiracy, but she stoutly maintains that though that book may not be genuine, it nevertheless shows the sort of thing of which the Jews are capable. Her book *Secret Societies and Subversive Movements* concludes: "For behind the concrete forces of revolution—whether Pan-German, Judaic or Illuminist—beyond that invisible secret circle which perhaps directs them all, is there not yet another force, still more potent, that must be taken into account? In looking back over the centuries at the dark episodes that have marked the history of the human race from its earliest origins—strange and horrible cults, waves of witchcraft, blasphemies and desecrations—how is it possible to ignore the existence of an Occult Power at work in the world? Individuals, sects, or races fired with the desire of world domination, have provided the fighting forces of destruction, but behind them are the veritable powers of darkness in eternal conflict with the powers of light."

I should describe Mrs. Nesta Webster as a perfectly sane and capable person with insane ideas, so widely do I disagree with her. I believe her influence has spread far beyond the circle of her actual readers. Milder forms of the same intellectual malaise at any rate are now very prevalent throughout the more prosperous classes in Great Britain and America. It is the only way to account for the behavior of Mr. Neville Chamberlain, for example, or Lord Rothermere, the British newspaper proprietor, towards the Jews, towards Russia, during the past two or three years. Mr. William Teeling again, to whom I refer in § 13, is another case. A tepid passive Christianity is becoming an aggressive pro-Christianity under the stresses of the time.

*Note* 12D. Sir Norman Angell and Mrs. Dorothy Frances Buxton, in a very clear and almost pressingly persuasive book, *You and the Refugee* (Penguin Books, 1939), argue for a practically unrestrained admission of these outcasts. They show in particular how beneficial a large refugee immigration might be to the British Empire. It would bring in new trades, new skill, find fresh work for the unemployed, and in Great Britain arrest the approaching decline in population—if that is desirable. Their plea for a more generous treatment of refugees, so far as assimilable individuals are concerned, is unanswerable.

But our authors' arguments for an inassimilable immigration *en bloc* are less convincing. That would only renew the trouble at a later date. There is no time to begin that old history again in new regions and among fresh difficulties. Disaster is advancing too rapidly upon our entire species. Jewish nationalism like every other nationalism must end and end soon. And even though the plea of existing unemployment is an irrational social barrier to assimilable immigrants, it is, in a country where the sense of social insecurity is growing, where confidence in the intelligence and good faith of the government is diminishing, and where large masses of the population, and especially the accumulation of untrained and unemployed young men, see no clear prospect of a tolerable life ahead, none the less a barrier. Implicitly the British authorities admit: "We do not know how to handle our own people, we are getting more and more bothered—by *everything*—and if these people come into our muddle, there is bound to be serious trouble." And so in effect they give them up to destruction, not outrageously and openly as the Germans do, but by looking in the opposite direction, and delaying action.

In a scientifically organized, forward-looking social order, there will be no people unemployed and there will be no difficulty whatever in the movement of population from point to point. The whole world will be everyman's and the fullness thereof. The bare possibility of such a rational order sustains whatever hope there is for mankind in this present survey of the human outlook. But this world we are living in is not a rational world and the harsh reality we have to face when we cast the Jewish horoscope is this closing-up of the avenues of escape.

Already in the past year or so, a multitude, scores and possibly hundreds of thousands, must have been done to death. And still it goes on. . . .

In *You and the Refugee,* however, I came upon one passage that affected me very disagreeably and I think I ought to say a word about it here. It is too germane to this discussion to omit:

"Not all Jews are Zionists, but all Jews will resent the letting down of Zionists, the surrender of Zionists to Arab terrorism. And their resentment will be world-wide. We do not perhaps realize the possible repercussions.

"The power of world Jewry is moral—the power of journalists, writers, dramatists, scientists. It is worth while for an Empire as gravely menaced as the British to have that power on its side." . . .

That is a threat and a very evil and embittering threat. Happily it is not made by Jews but by two overofficious Gentile champions on their behalf. I do not see things from the Imperialist standpoint of these authors. I think the British Empire has outlived its usefulness. But the consolidation of the English-speaking people as the vehicle of a world civilization is quite another matter, and a matter of great urgency. Yet unless the British government does what it is told in Palestine, the Chosen People, we are told, will devote themselves to preventing that consolidation. I think that is a very unhappy suggestion indeed. It does no justice to the intellectual quality of Israel. I doubt if any representative Jewish writer could be quoted in support of it. But it is exactly what the Jews are accused of doing by their worst enemies. My first reaction to it, until I realized that this dream of vindictive sabotage was a purely Gentile invention, was acute resentment and anger. I believe these two authors would be wise to take that tactless and unjustifiable passage out of any further editions of their well-intentioned book.

*Note* 13A. "We Catholics acknowledge readily, without any shame, nay with pride, that Catholicism cannot be identified simply and wholly with primitive Christianity, nor even with the Gospel of Christ, in the same way that the great oak cannot be identified with the tiny acorn. There is no mechanical identity, but an organic identity. And we go further and say that thousands of years hence Catholicism will probably be even richer, more luxuriant, more manifold in dogma, morals, law and worship, than the Catholicism of the present day. A religious historian of the fifth millennium A.D. will without difficulty discover in Catholicism conceptions and forms and practices which derive from India, China and Japan, and he will have to recognize a far more obvious 'complex of opposites.' It is quite true, Catholicism *is* a union of contraries. But 'contraries are not contradictories.' . . . The Gospel of Christ would have been no living gospel, and the seed which He scattered no living seed, if it had remained ever the tiny seed of A.D. 33, and not struck root, and had not assimilated foreign matter, and had not by the help of this foreign matter grown up into a tree, so that the birds of the air dwell in its branches." Professor Karl Adam, *The Spirit of Catholicism* (1938).

For reasons I have made perfectly clear in this book, I do not believe there will be any Roman Catholic Church at all in the fifth millennium A.D., but (see § 18) it is amusing to speculate how the successors of Professor Karl Adam, long before then, would have plaited into the Trinity that God of Male Sex Appeal from whose left eye sprang the Sun Goddess, while he blew Susa-no-o, the dragon-slaying Susa-no-o, from his nose. It is, I agree, not at all improbable, given the survival and continual growth of the Church.

Morgan Young, in the book I have cited in the text, tells that the great assimilation prophesied by Professor Karl Adam has already begun. The crude early Christians, still in the "acorn" phase, preferred martyrdom to burning a pinch of incense to the Roman God-Emperors, but the more catholic-spirited Church of today has already established friendly relations with the Shinto faith, Japan and Rome have exchanged envoys, and the Japanese Catholic bows in the Shinto temples in acquiescence to the local supremacy of the Emperor-Divinity over the Vatican.

*Note* 23A. Sir Arthur's *Epilogue* begins: "Shall we never pluck the best from fate and find the Golden Mean? Must we ever choose freedom without order, or order without freedom? Must justice and mercy bring always weakness in their train, and strength bring tyranny?

"Shall Peace be never made between equals, but imposed always by victor upon vanquished? Must every peace treaty sow the seeds of future war? Shall the strong never be magnanimous and the weak never secure justice? Must success always sap the will, and the humiliation of defeat incite only to revenge? Shall wars with changing victors be for ever the dire fate of men?

"We, the free democracies of the world, have the virtues bred and nursed in the pursuits of peace. That is not enough. We need also the sterner virtues—fortitude, daemonic energy, the will to act—and to act together." (p. 385.)

". . . willing cooperation and the endurance which is only possible to an instructed people who understand the purpose of their effort and approve it." (p. 384.) Sir Arthur Salter, *Security. Can We Retrieve It?* (1939).

END OF THE NOTES